THE SELECTED POEMS OF
ROY CAMPBELL

The Selected Poems of
ROY CAMPBELL

Chosen by Peter Alexander

Oxford New York Toronto Melbourne

OXFORD UNIVERSITY PRESS

1982

Oxford University Press, Walton Street, Oxford OX2 6DP

London Glasgow New York Toronto
Delhi Bombay Calcutta Madras Karachi
Kuala Lumpur Singapore Hong Kong Tokyo
Nairobi Dar es Salaam Cape Town
Melbourne Auckland

and associate companies in
Beirut Berlin Ibadan Mexico City

British Library Cataloguing in Publication Data
Campbell, Roy
The selected poems of Roy Campbell
I. Title II. Alexander, Peter
821   PR9368.C/
ISBN 0–19–211946–X

Library of Congress Cataloging in Publication Data
Campbell, Roy, 1901–1957.
The selected poems of Roy Campbell.
Bibliography: p.
Includes indexes.
I. Alexander, Peter (Peter F.) II. Title.
PR9369.3.C35A6   1982   821   81–22338
ISBN 0–19–211946–X   AACR2

Set by Western Printing Services Ltd
Printed in Great Britain
at the University Press, Oxford
by Eric Buckley
Printer to the University

To Christine

CONTENTS

INTRODUCTION

MANY prolific poets show to advantage in selections which screen out their inferior work, and Roy Campbell is certainly among them. The quality of his work was always very uneven. His major poems, *The Flaming Terrapin*, *The Wayzgoose*, *The Georgiad*, and *Flowering Rifle*, have long barren passages, and even his volumes of short lyric poems include a significant number of verses that scarcely rise above the level of doggerel. Yet at his best he produced satire deadly in its effectiveness, and lyrics of a sensuous beauty scarcely matched in the twentieth century. It is not surprising, then, that several editors have set out to present the best of his work in selected editions. Campbell himself produced three such volumes (*Sons of the Mistral*, *Collected Poems*, and *Collected Poems* II), and such distinguished editors as Uys Krige and Joseph Lalley have produced fine selections. At least one other selection is shortly to be published.

The present selection of Campbell's poems differs from all others in being arranged chronologically by the dates of the poems' composition. This arrangement has the obvious advantage of allowing the reader to study Campbell's poetic development, and it seems likely that previous editors have not adopted the chronological arrangement chiefly because of the extreme difficulty of establishing the dates of composition of Campbell's work.

His output of original poems can be divided into phases, marked by alterations, more or less distinct, in tone, style, and subject-matter. Though there is an obvious danger in seeking simple parallels between any poet's life and work, there do appear to be clear connections between major changes in Campbell's life and simultaneous developments in his poetry. For this reason it is helpful to summarize the chief events in his extraordinary career.

He was born in Durban, South Africa, on 2 October 1901, the third son of a wealthy doctor. His childhood was of the wild and free-ranging kind most children only dream about; he was provided with horses, guns, buck to shoot, fish to catch, and great areas of country in which to range freely. To this upbringing he later attributed his enthusiasm for physical pursuits, his love of energy, violence, and colour, and his dislike of modern, urban life. In fact, however, his contemporaries remember him as a solitary book-worm, less interested in hunting than in poetry. To this period belongs the juvenile verse, written before 1919, derivative of Scott, Burns, Shelley, early Yeats, and of the Anglo-Canadian poet Robert Service.

Campbell left the Durban Boys' High School in 1917, and after a year at Natal University College in Pietermaritzburg he sailed for England at the end of the First World War, to try to enter Merton College, Oxford, intending to read English. He did very little formal work, however, concentrating instead on his own poetry, and read-ing voraciously such writers as Wyndham Lewis, the Sitwells, and T. S. Eliot. Abandoning his attempt to enter Oxford, he tramped around southern France during 1920, taking odd labouring jobs and returning to London at intervals. It was in London in October 1921 that he met a beautiful girl named Mary Garman, whom he married in February the next year. The couple rented a converted cowshed in Aberdaron in West Wales, where Campbell finished his first major poem, *The Flaming Terrapin*, which he published in 1924. *The Flaming Terrapin* is representative of the image-choked over-energetic verse of Campbell's early period, which lasted until 1925.

Campbell returned to South Africa in 1924 and during 1926, in collaboration with William Plomer and Laurens van der Post, edited a bilingual literary magazine, *Voorslag*. A quarrel with the financial backers of *Voorslag*, from which Campbell resigned after the second issue, combined with a growing dislike of South Africa's political climate, drove Campbell to return to Europe. The African poems which he wrote in 1926, however, mark the beginning of the mature work he produced with a cascading wealth of invention until the mid-1930s. To this mature period belong also the two major satires, *The Wayzgoose* and *The Georgiad*, a sense of persecution having been awakened in Campbell by his setbacks in South Africa and by the lesbian love-affair which Mary Campbell had during 1927 with Vita Sackville-West, whose guests the Campbells were for some months in Kent.

From 1928 until 1941 they lived in France and in Spain, and Campbell's love of southern Europe is everywhere apparent in his work during this period. His slow conversion to Catholicism bet-ween 1933 and 1935 marks another change in his writing; this change is reflected in the obscurity of the 'Mithraic Emblems' se-quence, the religious commitment of many of the lyrics, and the increasing shrillness of the satirical pieces; the uneven quality of the verse he produced from this period until the end of his life is very marked. He was not unaware of this decline, and it is significant that from the mid-1930s he wrote less original poetry, choosing instead to devote himself to translations as his creative powers slowly waned.

His emotional involvement in the Spanish Civil War is evident in many of the poems written after 1936; several reflect his direct experience of the fighting in Toledo, where he was living when the war broke out. His sympathies were with the Nationalists, though he never fought for them as he claimed to have done.

He joined the British Army in 1942, and served in East Africa, first in training with Wingate's commando force and then, after being disabled, as a coast-watcher for German submarines. After the war he worked as a clerk on the War Damage Commission in London before joining the BBC as a Talks Producer. For a short period he edited an unsuccessful magazine, *The Catacomb*. During the last years of his life, from 1952, he lived in Portugal, where he was killed in a car crash on 23 April 1957.

It would be a mistake to assert that the phases of Campbell's writing are clear-cut, for the changes in his work are neither immediate nor absolute. Shifts of tone and subject-matter are, however, evident. The course of his creative life can only be followed if a chronologically arranged edition of the poems is available, and Campbell seems to have been aware of this. He would have preferred to collect his own poems in chronological order; he disliked the first volume of *Collected Poems*, in which the work was divided into 'lyrics' and 'satires', and in *Collected Poems* II, over which he had much more control, he produced a roughly chronological arrangement, dividing the work into 'early' and 'later' poems, though he was too vague about dates to make the arrangement very accurate.

All attempts to establish dates of composition of Campbell's poems must be to some extent speculative, since except for one period of four days in March 1957 he kept no diary, he very seldom dated his letters, and he seems never to have dated the manuscripts of his poems. The dates appended to poems in this volume have been arrived at by five principal methods, and it is worth summarizing these briefly. Especially during the 1930s, there are direct references in Campbell's letters to poems as having been 'just written'; more rarely Campbell would include the draft of a new poem in the text of his letter. More rarely still he includes a prose summary of the whole or part of a newly-written poem in his letters. In these cases, where the letter can be dated, the approximate date of composition of the poem can be established. Secondly, in 1947 an aspiring biographer wrote asking for the dates of many poems; Campbell's reply is useful in dating some of the poems he had recently produced. Thirdly, his longer poems occasionally make references to contemporary events which can be dated, as when in *Flowering Rifle* he refers to having 'today' heard of the sinking of the Nationalist warship the *Baleares*, which foundered on 6 March 1938. Fourthly there are the accounts of his contemporaries, some of whom recorded the dates of composition of his poems: William Plomer, for instance, noted the exact dates of composition of many of Campbell's African poems of 1926, and another close friend did so during Campbell's last years. Fifthly, close examination of the handwriting, paper, and ink of poem-manuscripts allows one to relate undated poems to letters, or to manuscripts of dated poems. This is of particular importance with the longer works; it was possible for instance to establish the approximate dates of various sections of *Flowering Rifle* because of the changes in paper size and in the colours of the inks Campbell used during the period of the poem's composition.*

In the case of those poems where no information on dating could be found, the date of first publication in volume-form must serve as a rough guide. It will be noticed, however, that the great bulk of these undated poems are from the volume Campbell called *Flowering Reeds* (1933); and since it is clear from Campbell's correspondence that he had published in his previous volume, *Adamastor* (1930) all the poems he then had ready, the *Flowering Reeds* poems must all have been completed during the 30-month period between the publication dates of these two volumes.

I have thought it right to depart from the chronological arrangement, so far as it can be established, in the sole instance of the 'Mithraic Emblems' sequence (from the volume of the same title) where the meaning of the poems would be obscured by disrupting the order in which Campbell finally printed them. In addition it has proved very difficult to date Campbell's many translations from Latin, French, Spanish, and Portuguese. I have distinguished transla-

---

* Readers interested in the dating of particular poems will find the details in Peter Alexander, *Roy Campbell: A Critical Biography* (Oxford University Press, 1982).

tions from original poems as far as possible by grouping the former in a separate section at the end of this volume.

The choice of text is a difficult one with Campbell's work, for he reprinted many of his poems several times, making textual changes. Occasionally he would recast a poem entirely, dropping several stanzas, as with 'A Jug of Water', or even breaking one poem into two, as he did with *Flowering Rifle*. When his manuscripts survive the problems are often compounded, since he produced many draft variants of poems. I have chosen to use always the most recent form of any poem published in Campbell's lifetime, on the assumption that it embodies Campbell's considered judgement. Even this course poses problems with those poems last published in the first volume of *Collected Poems*, since Campbell did not oversee its production. I have compared all such poems with the text of the volumes in which Campbell originally printed them in the hope of weeding out printer's errors, and I have also checked the text against as many of the original manuscripts as are known to be extant.

In the production of this edition I have been greatly helped by detailed biographical information provided by the poet's late widow, Mary Campbell, and by his daughter Teresa. I have been immeasurably helped by the labours of two previous scholars, the late Professor W. H. Gardner, and Mr Alan Paton. I have also profited by discussions with Mrs Marcia Leveson.

My sincere thanks are due to the staff of the following libraries, which gave me prompt and courteous assistance: The British Library; Cornell University Library; Cambridge University Library; The Johannesburg City Library; Durban City Library; The Killie Campbell Africana Library; Witwatersrand University Library; The South African National Library; The Corey Library, Rhodes University; The University of Saskatchewan Library, Saskatoon; Washington University Library; The Library of the Humanities Research Center, University of Texas at Austin; and The University of Cape Town Library.

I wish to thank the following for permission to quote copyright material: Curtis Brown Ltd. for lines from *Flowering Rifle* and poems from *Adamastor*; Jonathan Cape Ltd. and the Executors of the Roy Campbell Estate for lines from *The Wayzgoose* and *The Flaming Terrapin*; Faber & Faber Ltd. for poems from *Talking Bronco*; and Hughes Massie Ltd. and The Harvill Press for poems from *St John of the Cross* and Baudelaire's *Poems: A Translation of Les Fleurs du Mal.*

I have been greatly aided in the gathering of information by generous financial help from the Australian Academy of the Humanities, which enabled me to undertake an extensive tour of libraries with collections of Campbell's manuscripts.

PFA

University of New South Wales
July 1981

CAMPBELL'S PRINCIPAL WORKS

Light on a Dark Horse (London, Hollis & Carter, 1951)
Lorca (Cambridge, Bowes & Bowes, 1952)
The Mamba's Precipice (London, Frederick Muller, 1953)
Portugal (London, Max Reinhardt, 1957)

ROY CAMPBELL 1901–1957
A Chronology

1901   Born in Durban, 2 October

1906   Zulu Rebellion

1910   Sent to Durban Boys' High School

1916   Attempts unsuccessfully to join the Army

1917   Matriculates with third-class pass

1918   Takes English, Physics, Botany at Natal University College. Sails for England late *December*

1919   Rents rooms in Oxford, studies for Responsions. Visits Paris, Germany *June–August*

1920   Abandons studies, tramps around southern Europe

1921   Returns to London *September*. Meets Mary Garman *October*

1922   Marries Mary Garman *11 February*. Moves to Aberdaron, Wales. Daughter Teresa born *November*

1923   Moves back to London *?June*

1924   Returns to South Africa *June*. Mary and Teresa join him *December*

1925   Living in Peace Cottage; to Sezela (north of Durban) *mid-April*. Meets William Plomer *June*

1926   Daughter Anna born *March*. Plomer joins them at Sezela *May*. *Voorslag* appears June and July. RC resigns from *Voorslag* *25 July*. Sails for England *December*

1927   Settles in Sevenoaks Weald, Kent, late *April*. The Campbells meet Vita Sackville-West late *May*; move into Vita's cottage *1 October*. Mary tells RC of her affair with Vita early *November*

1928   RC leaves for France *April*. Mary joins him *?June*

1929   Living in Provence, occasional visits to London

1930   Wyndham Lewis visits RC in Provence *mid-July*

1931   Provence

1932   Uys Krige first visits RC *October*. Mary's affair with Jeanne, RC's with Lisa

1933   Final break with Plomer *August*. Move to Spain *November*

1934   Living in Barcelona; move to Valencia *March*, and to Altea *May*

1935   Received into Roman Catholic Church *June*. To Toledo late *June*

1936   Riots *March*; RC beaten and arrested by Assault Guards *16 March*.
       Civil War begins *18 July*. Fighting in Toledo from *20 July*. Camp-
       bells flee Toledo late *July*; arrive England *11 August*; live in Arundel,
       Sussex

1937   Sails to Portugal *29 January*. Settles in Cezimbra early February. RC
       tours Spanish battlefields *July*. Settles in Estombar *September*

1938   To Rome *September*

1939   Tours Italy *January–March*; returns to Toledo *April*. Franco's Vic-
       tory Parade *19 May*. Britain at war *3 September*

1940   Acting as British 'secret agent'

1941   To London by sea *August*; becomes Air Raid Precautions warden.
       Mary and daughters join him by air *December*

1942   Joins British Army *1 April*; trains in Wales, Winchester, Yorkshire,
       Derbyshire

1943   Embarks for Africa, troop-ship breaks down *February*. Re-embarks
       24 March. On leave in Durban *April*. Overland to Nairobi *18
       April–5 May*. Transferred to Wingate's force *June*; injures hip *June*.
       Coast-watcher from *September*

1944   Returns to England *June*. Joins War Damage Commission *Novem-
       ber*

1945   Resigns War Damage Commission *21 July*

1946   Joins BBC *1 January*

1947   Living in London, working for BBC

1948   Working for BBC; lecturing in Spain *October*

1949   Resigns BBC *September*, begins editing *The Catacomb*

1950   Holiday in France *May–September*

1951   Living in London, lecturing in Spain *May* and *October–December*.
       The Catacomb suspends publication *December*

1952   Moves to Sintra, Portugal *May*

1953   Lecture-tour of North America *October–December*

1954   Awarded honorary doctorate by Natal University *March*; tours
       Mozambique *March*.

1955   Second lecture-tour of North America *October–December*

1956   Moves from Sintra to Linhó *April*

1957   Death in car crash *23 April*

NOTE

The date of composition where known is given at the end of each poem, followed by the abbreviated title of the volume in which the poem was published. Dates of volume publication can be found in the list of Campbell's Principal Works (p. xvii).

The following abbreviations have been used:

A	*Adamastor*
Baudelaire	*Poems: A Translation of Les Fleurs du Mal*
CP I, CP II, CP III	*Collected Poems*, Volumes I, II, III
FR	*Flowering Reeds*
ME	*Mithraic Emblems*
P	*Poems*
St John	*The Poems of Saint John of the Cross*
SM	*Sons of the Mistral*
TB	*Talking Bronco*

ORIGINAL POEMS

The Theology of Bongwi, the Baboon

THIS is the wisdom of the Ape
    Who yelps beneath the Moon—
'Tis God who made me in His shape
    He is a Great Baboon.
'Tis He who tilts the moon askew   5
    And fans the forest trees,
The heavens which are broad and blue
    Provide him his trapeze;
He swings with tail divinely bent
    Around those azure bars   10
And munches to his Soul's content
    The kernels of the stars;
And when I die, His loving care
    Will raise me from the sod
To learn the perfect Mischief there,   15
    The Nimbleness of God.

                    [1918. A, CP I]

Selection from The Flaming Terrapin

SKITTLES to Noah's axe, the great trunks sprawled,
And with the weight of their own bodies hauled
Their screaming roots from earth: their tall green towers
Tilted, and at a sudden crack came down   215
With roaring cataracts of leaves and flowers
To crush themselves upon the rocks, and drown
The earth for acres in their leafy flood;
Heaped up and gashed and toppled in the mud,
Their coloured fruits poured forth their juicy gore   220
To make sweet shambles of the grassy floor.

When star by star, above the vaulted hill,
The sky poured out its hoarded bins of gold,
Night stooped upon the mountain-tops, and still
Those low concussions from the forest rolled,   225
And still more fiercely hounded by their dread
Lost in the wastes the savage tribesmen fled.

Out of its orbit sags the cratered sun
And strews its last red cinders on the land,
The hurricanes of chaos have begun   230
To buzz like hornets on the shifting sand.
Across the swamp the surly day goes down,
Voracious insects rise on wings that drone,
Stormed in a fog to where the mountains frown,
Locked in their tetanous agonies of stone.   235
The cold and plaintive jackals of the wind
Whine on the great waste levels of the sea,
And like a leper, faint and tatter-skinned,
The wan moon makes a ghost of every tree.

The Ark is launched; cupped by the streaming breeze,   240
The stiff sails tug the long reluctant keel,
And Noah, spattered by the rising seas,
Stands with his great fist fastened to the wheel.
Like driven clouds, the waves went rustling by,
Feathered and fanned across their liquid sky,   245
And, like those waves, the clouds in silver bars
Creamed on the scattered shingle of the stars.
All night he watched black water coil and burn,
And the white wake of phosphorus astern
Lit up the sails and made the lanterns dim,   250
Until it seemed the whole sea burned for him;
Beside the keel he saw the grey sharks move,
And the long lines of fire their fins would groove,
Seemed each a ghost that followed in its sleep
Those long phantasmal coffins of the deep;   255
And in that death-light, as the long swell rolled,
The tarpon was a thunderbolt of gold.

Then in the long night-watches he would hear
The whinnying stallions of the wind career.
And to their lost companions, in their flight,   260
Whine like forlorn cicalas through the night.

By day the sky put on a peacock dress,
And, from its far bewildering recess,
Snowed its white birds about the rolling hull—
The swift sea-swallow and the veering gull   265
Mixed in a mist of circling wings, whose swoops
Haloed her with a thousand silver hoops;
And from the blue waves, startled in a swarm,
On sunlit wings, butterflies of the storm!
The flying-fishes in their silver mail   270
Rose up like stars, and pattered down like hail,
While the blunt whale, ponderous in his glee,
Churned his broad flukes and siphoned up the sea,
And through it, as the creamy circles spread,
Heaved the superb Olympus of his head.   275

Then far away, all in a curve of gold,
Flounced round with spray and frilled with curling foam,
Cleaving the ocean's flatness with its bold
Ridges of glory, rose a towering dome
As the great Terrapin, bulking on high,   280
Spread forth his huge dimensions on the sky.
Not even Teneriffe, that awful dyke,
When the sun strikes him silver to the spike,
Sends such a glory through his cloudy spray
As did the Flaming Terrapin that day,   285
Rushing to meet the Ark; with such a sweep
The blue Zambezi rumbles to the deep,
With such a roar white avalanches slide
To strip whole forests from a mountain's side.
But Noah drew his blunt stone anchor in   290
And heaved it at him; with a thund'rous din
The stony fluke impaled the brazen shell
And set it clanging like a surly bell.
Its impact woke the looped and lazy chain
And rattling swiftly out across the main,   295

Drawn by the anchor from its dark abode,
Into the light that glittering serpent flowed
Chafing the waves: then as a mustang colt,
Feeling the snaffle, lurches for a bolt—
With such a lurch, with such a frantic rear,   300
The Ark lunged forward on her mad career,
And the old Captain, with a grip of steel,
Laid his brown hands once more upon the wheel,
Bidding his joyous pilot haul him free
From the dead earth to dare the living sea!   305
Rowelled by that sharp prow to hissing hate,
The waves washed round her in a dreary spate,
And, as she passed, with slow vindictive swoop
Swerved in to gnash their teeth against the poop:
But like torn Hectors at the chariot wheel,   310
She dragged their mangled ruins with her keel:
Till puffed by growing rage to greater height,
Their foamy summits towered into the night
So steeply, that it seemed by God's decree
The Alps had all gone marching on the sea,   315
Or Andes had been liquefied and rolled
Their moonlit ridges in a surf of gold!

[1921–3. Published 1924, and in *CP* I]

Lines from *The Golden Shower*

The drought is done. Now to their gusty games,
Tagging their nimble heels with fleeter flames
Than those with which they charred the winter grass,*   140
The winds upon the tops of lilies pass.
New sources rimple from the mountain-roots
And drawn in silver leashes by the spruits
Long files of red-gold lilies wind and meet
To spoor the rovings of their crystal feet: 145

* This refers to the annual (and suicidal) burning of the grass throughout Africa by the natives. [RC]

The marshes, where the yellow weavers breed,
Whirr with great gusts of gold, and as they swing,
Shrill on the bending rushes, every reed
Lights its frail taper with a burnished wing.
Here, where relumed by changing season, burn   150
The phoenix trees of Africa in turn,
Each from the other's ashes taking fire
As swiftly to revive as to expire,
Mimosa, jacaranda, kaffirboom,
And tulip-tree, igniting bloom from bloom,   155
While through their zodiac of flowery signs
The flame-furred sun like some huge moth is whirled
Circling forever, as he fades or shines,
Around the open blossom of the world—
All things as if to Venus' touch ignite   160
And the grey soil is tinder to her tread
Whence married flowers explode into the light—
And burn with fiery pollen as they wed.
She burns through bark and wood as flame through glass
The dust is fuel to her warm desire   165
On which, with scintillating plumes, the grass
Runs waving like a disembodied fire:
But we of all her splendours are most splendid
In whom the rest are held and comprehended,
And our clear sprites, whom rays and showers begem,   170
Burn through each other as the world through them.

Though we seem merely mortal, what we are,
Is clearly mirrored on a deathless flood.
We change and fade: our dust is strewn afar—
Only the ancient river of our blood,   175
Rising far-off in unimagined spaces,
Red with the silt and ruin of the past
And churning with the strife of savage races,
Like deep Zambezi goes on rolling past,
Swiftens through us its energies unending,   180
And reaches out, beneath the shades we cast,
To what vast ocean of the night descending
Or in what sunny lake at last to sleep,

We do not know—save that it turns to foam,
Just here, for us; its currents curl and comb   185
And all its castalies in thunder leap,
Silvering, forth into a white resilience
Of ecstacy, whose momentary brilliance
Must compensate eternities of sleep.
Knowing these things, are not we lovers, then,   190
Though mortal in our nature, more than men?
Since by our senses, as by rivers, veined,
The hills of primal memory are drained,
And the dim summits of their frosty spars,
Whose tops are nibbled by the grazing stars,   195
Thawed by the rising noon of our desire,
And fusing into consciousness and fire,
Down through the sounding canyons of the soul
Their rich alluvium of starlight roll.

We bear to future times the secret news   200
That first was whispered to the new-made earth:
We are like worlds with nations in our thews,
Shaped for delight, and primed for endless birth.
We never kiss but vaster shapes possess
Our bodies: towering up into the skies,   205
We wear the night and thunder for our dress,
While, vaster than imagination, rise
Two giant forms, like cobras flexed to sting,
Bending their spines in one tremendous ring
With all the starlight burning through their eyes,   210
Fire in their loins, and on their lips the hiss
Of breath indrawn above some steep abyss.
When, like the sun, our heavenly desire
Has turned this flesh into a cloud of fire
Through which our nerves their strenuous lightnings fork,
Eternity has blossomed in an hour   216
And as we gaze upon that wondrous flower
We think the world a beetle on its stalk.

[1925. Recast for *CP* II]

6

Mazeppa

To Catherine Macdonald Maclean

HELPLESS, condemned, yet still for mercy croaking
Like a trussed rooster swinging by the claws,
They hoisted him: they racked his joints asunder;
They lashed his belly to a thing of thunder—
A tameless brute, with hate and terror smoking,   5
That never felt the bit between its jaws.

So when his last vain struggle had subsided,
His gleeful butchers wearied of the fun:
Looping the knots about his thighs and back,
With lewd guffaws they heard his sinews crack,   10
And laughed to see his lips with foam divided,
His eyes too glazed with blood to know the sun.

A whip cracked, they were gone: alone they followed
The endless plain: the long day volleyed past
With only the white clouds above them speeding   15
And the grey steppe into itself receding,
Where each horizon, by a vaster swallowed,
Repeated but the bareness of the last.

Out of his trance he wakened: on they flew:
The blood ran thumping down into his brain: 20
With skull a-dangle, facing to the sky
That like a great black wind went howling by,
Foaming, he strove to gnash the tethers through
That screwed his flesh into a knot of pain.

To him the earth and sky were drunken things—   25
Bucked from his senses, jolted to and fro,
He only saw them reeling hugely past,
As sees a sailor soaring at the mast,
Who retches as his sickening orbit swings
The sea above him and the sky below.   30

Into his swelling veins and open scars
The python cords bit deeper than before,
And the great beast, to feel their sharpened sting,
Looping his body in a thundrous sling
As if to jolt his burden to the stars, 35
Recoiled, and reared, and plunged ahead once more.

Three days had passed, yet could not check nor tire
That cyclone whirling in its spire of sand:
Charged with resounding cordite, as they broke
In sudden flashes through the flying smoke, 40
The fusillading hoofs in rapid fire
Rumbled a dreary volley through the land.

Now the dark sky with gathering ravens hums:
And vultures, swooping down on his despair,
Struck at the loose and lolling head whereunder 45
The flying coffin sped, the hearse of thunder,
Whose hoof-beats with the roll of muffled drums
Led on the black processions of the air.

The fourth sun saw the great black wings descending
Where crashed in blood and spume the charger lay: 50
From the snapped cords a shapeless bundle falls—
Scarce human now, like a cut worm he crawls
Still with a shattered arm his face defending
As inch by inch he drags himself away.

Who'd give a penny for that strip of leather? 55
Go, set him flapping in a field of wheat,
Or take him as a pull-through for your gun,
Or hang him up to kipper in the sun,
Or leave him here, a strop to hone the weather
And whet the edges of the wind and sleet. 60

Who on that brow foresees the gems aglow?
Who, in that shrivelled hand, the sword that swings
Wide as a moonbeam through the farthest regions,
To crop the blood-red harvest of the legions,
Making amends to every cheated crow 65
And feasting vultures on the fat of kings.

8

This is that Tartar prince, superbly pearled,
Whose glory soon on every wind shall fly,
Whose arm shall wheel the nations into battle,
Whose warcry, rounding up the tribes like cattle,   70
Shall hurl his cossacks rumbling through the world
As thunder hurls the hail-storm through the sky.

And so it is whenever some new god,
Boastful, and young, and avid of renown,
Would make his presence known upon the earth—   75
Choosing some wretch from those of mortal birth,
He takes his body like a helpless clod
And on the croup of genius straps it down.

With unseen hand he knots the cord of pain,
Unseen the winged courser strains for flight: 80
He leads it forth into some peopled space
Where the dull eyes of those who throng the place
See not the wings that wave, the thews that strain,
But only mark the victim of their might.

Left for the passing rabble to admire,   85
He fights for breath, he chokes, and rolls his eyes:
They mime his agonies with loud guffaws,
They pelt him from the place with muddy paws,
Nor do they hear the sudden snort of fire
To which the tether snaps, the great wings rise. . . .   90

Vertiginously through the heavens rearing,
Plunging through chasms of eternal pain,
Splendours and horrors open on his view,
And wingèd fiends like fiercer kites pursue,
With hateful patience at his side careering,   95
To hook their claws of iron on his brain.

With their green eyes his solitude is starlit,
That lamp the dark and lurk in every brier:
He sinks obscure into the night of sorrow
To rise again, refulgent on the morrow,   100
With eagles for his ensigns, and the scarlet
Horizon for his Rubicon of fire.

9

Out of his pain, perhaps, some god-like thing,
Is born. A god has touched him, though with whips:
We only know that, hooted from our walls,   105
He hurtles on his way, he reels, he falls,
And staggers up to find himself a king
With truth a silver trumpet at his lips.

[Begun 1921, completed 1926. A, SM, CP I]

Solo and Chorus from 'The Conquistador'

Solo   COME, we are hungry; bake us bread,
Great sun: you torrents, grind the flour:
Nuggets of gold and rubies red,
Sprinkle the buns that we devour:
Bring the great rocks from ovens dark,   5
Digest the grim diluvial cakes—
The old ships-biscuits of the Ark,
The cookery of seas and lakes.
Chorus   *O bake us the red, the blue,*
The boulders of the broad Karroo.   10

Solo   The sun eats mud and fire: in sleep
We hanker for such foods, alas,
Our thoughts like flocks of springbok sweep
The vastitudes of bitter grass:
With rasp of roots our pasture creaks,   15
Tugging harsh stems our tongues are curled—
Come quit these pastures for the peaks
Before we devastate the world.
Chorus   *Not while so green a salad fills*
The blue bowl of the circling hills.   20

Solo   Up there, the sun on grills of gold
Fries the red clouds for you and me,
The huge cooks of the whirlwind scold
And on their spits revolve the free,

Roast phoenixes, for all who ask, 25
With battered breast and frizzled legs—
Then leave your dull prosaic task
And feast upon the angels' eggs!
Chorus   *Our farms are ringed with peaceful trees*
         Where fatter poultry roost than these. 30

Solo   The frisky gnus that gallop there
       And kick their heels into the sky,
       Singed by the stars, with tails aflare,
       Stampede across the mountains high:
       They'll fire the grass, they'll char the roots 35
       And bring a famine on the herds—
       We strove to pacify the brutes,
       It was too late to bandy words.
Chorus   *No more these rolling plains, O chief,*
         Shall thunder under tons of beef. 40

Solo   O sound the sanguinary drums
       As to the North our rule extends,
       And if you do not trust your guns,
       Diplomacy will gain your ends:
       Recall the fights your fathers won 45
       Against such odds, in such a fix—
       The rattle of the maxim-gun
       Against the clattering of sticks.
Chorus   *When the hurly-burly's done*
         Let smoke and thunder quench the sun. 50

Solo   Then fly, my wolf-pack, on before,
       Swift in your pilgrimage of hope,
       And I shall follow on your spoor
       To kiss the bunions of the Pope:
       A thousand priests, behind our thunder, 55
       Shall follow with the crow and kite,
       To cure the wounds of those we plunder
       With words of mercy, hope, and light!

[1926. A, CP I]

The Serf

HIS naked skin clothed in the torrid mist
That puffs in smoke around the patient hooves,
The ploughman drives, a slow somnambulist,
And through the green his crimson furrow grooves.
His heart, more deeply than he wounds the plain,   5
Long by the rasping share of insult torn,
Red clod, to which the war-cry once was rain
And tribal spears the fatal sheaves of corn,
Lies fallow now. But as the turf divides
I see in the slow progress of his strides   10
Over the toppled clods and falling flowers,
The timeless, surly patience of the serf
That moves the nearest to the naked earth
And ploughs down palaces, and thrones, and towers.

[28 July 1926. *A, SM, CP* I]

The Zulu Girl

To F. C. Slater

WHEN in the sun the hot red acres smoulder,
Down where the sweating gang its labour plies,
A girl flings down her hoe, and from her shoulder
Unslings her child tormented by the flies.

She takes him to a ring of shadow pooled   5
By thorn-trees: purpled with the blood of ticks,
While her sharp nails, in slow caresses ruled,
Prowl through his hair with sharp electric clicks,

His sleepy mouth, plugged by the heavy nipple,
Tugs like a puppy, grunting as he feeds: 10
Through his frail nerves her own deep languors ripple
Like a broad river sighing through its reeds.

12

Yet in that drowsy stream his flesh imbibes
An old unquenched unsmotherable heat—
The curbed ferocity of beaten tribes,   15
The sullen dignity of their defeat.

Her body looms above him like a hill
Within whose shade a village lies at rest,
Or the first cloud so terrible and still
That bears the coming harvest in its breast.   20

[July 1926. *A, SM, CP* I]

The Making of a Poet

IN every herd there is some restive steer
Who leaps the cows and heads each hot stampede,
Till the old bulls unite in jealous fear
To hunt him from the pastures where they feed.

Lost in the night he hears the jungles crash   5
And desperately, lest his courage fail,
Across his hollow flanks with sounding lash
Scourges the heavy whipcord of his tail.

Far from the phalanxes of horns that ward
The sleeping herds he keeps the wolf at bay,   10
At nightfall by the slinking leopard spoored,
And goaded by the fly-swarm through the day.

31 July 1926. *A, SM, CP* I]

To a Pet Cobra

WITH breath indrawn and every nerve alert,
As at the brink of some profound abyss,
I love on my bare arm, capricious flirt,
To feel the chilly and incisive kiss

13

Of your lithe tongue that forks its swift caress   5
Between the folded slumber of your fangs,
And half reveals the nacreous recess
Where death upon those dainty hinges hangs.

Our lonely lives in every chance agreeing,
It is no common friendship that you bring,   10
It was the desert starved us into being,
The hate of men that sharpened us to sting:
Sired by starvation, suckled by neglect,
Hate was the surly tutor of our youth:
I too can hiss the hair of men erect   15
Because my lips are venomous with truth.

Where the hard rock is barren, scorched the spring,
Shrivelled the grass, and the hot wind of death
Hornets the crag with whirred metallic wing—
We drew the fatal secret of our breath: 20
By whirlwinds bugled forth, whose funnelled suction
Scrolls the spun sand into a golden spire,
Our spirits leaped, hosannas of destruction,
Like desert lilies forked with tongues of fire.

Dainty one, deadly one, whose folds are panthered   25
With stars, my slender Kalihari flower,
Whose lips with fangs are delicately anthered,
Whose coils are volted with electric power,
I love to think how men of my dull nation
Might spurn your sleep with inadvertent heel   30
To kindle up the lithe retaliation
And caper to the slash of sudden steel.

There is no sea so wide, no waste so steril
But holds a rapture for the sons of strife:
There shines upon the topmost peak of peril   35
A throne for spirits that abound in life:
There is no joy like theirs who fight alone,
Whom lust or gluttony have never tied,
Who in their purity have built a throne,
And in their solitude a tower of pride.   40

I wish my life, O suave and silent sphinx,
Might flow like yours in some such strenuous line,
My days the scales, my years the bony links
That chain the length of its resilient spine:
And when at last the moment comes to strike,   45
Such venom give my hilted fangs the power,
Like drilling roots the dirty soil that spike,
To sting these rotted wastes into a flower.

[31 July 1926. *A, SM, CP* I]

Tristan da Cunha

To Robert Lyle

SNORE in the foam; the night is vast and blind;
The blanket of the mist about your shoulders,
Sleep your old sleep of rock, snore in the wind,
Snore in the spray! the storm your slumber lulls,
His wings are folded on your nest of boulders   5
As on their eggs the grey wings of your gulls.

No more as when, so dark an age ago,
You hissed a giant cinder from the ocean,
Around your rocks you furl the shawling snow
Half sunk in your own darkness, vast and grim,   10
And round you on the deep with surly motion
Pivot your league-long shadow as you swim.

Why should you haunt me thus but that I know
My surly heart is in your own displayed,
Round whom such leagues in endless circuit flow,   15
Whose hours in such a gloomy compass run—
A dial with its league-long arm of shade
Slowly revolving to the moon and sun.

My pride has sunk, like your grey fissured crags,
By its own strength o'ertoppled and betrayed: 20
I, too, have burned the wind with fiery flags
Who now am but a roost for empty words,
An island of the sea whose only trade
Is in the voyages of its wandering birds.

Did you not, when your strength became your pyre   25
Deposed and tumbled from your flaming tower,
Awake in gloom from whence you sank in fire,
To find, Antaeus-like, more vastly grown,
A throne in your own darkness, and a power
Sheathed in the very coldness of your stone?   30

Your strength is that you have no hope or fear,
You march before the world without a crown,
The nations call you back, you do not hear,
The cities of the earth grow grey behind you,
You will be there when their great flames go down   35
And still the morning in the van will find you.

You march before the continents, you scout
In front of all the earth; alone you scale
The mast-head of the world, a lorn look-out,
Waving the snowy flutter of your spray   40
And gazing back in infinite farewell
To suns that sink and shores that fade away.

From your grey tower what long regrets you fling
To where, along the low horizon burning,
The great swan-breasted seraphs soar and sing,   45
And suns go down, and trailing splendours dwindle,
And sails on lonely errands unreturning
Glow with a gold no sunrise can rekindle.

Turn to the night; these flames are not for you
Whose steeple for the thunder swings its bells;   50
Grey Memnon, to the tempest only true,
Turn to the night, turn to the shadowing foam,
And let your voice, the saddest of farewells,
With sullen curfew toll the grey wings home.

16

The wind, your mournful syren, haunts the gloom;   55
The rocks, spray-clouded, are your signal guns
Whose stony nitre, puffed with flying spume,
Rolls forth in grim salute your broadside hollow
Over the gorgeous burials of suns
To sound the tocsin of the storms that follow.   60

Plunge forward like a ship to battle hurled,
Slip the long cables of the failing light,
The level rays that moor you to the world:
Sheathed in your armour of eternal frost,
Plunge forward, in the thunder of the fight   65
To lose yourself as I would fain be lost.

Exiled like you and severed from my race
By the cold ocean of my own disdain,
Do I not freeze in such a wintry space,
Do I not travel through a storm as vast   70
And rise at times, victorious from the main,
To fly the sunrise at my shattered mast?

Your path is but a desert where you reap
Only the bitter knowledge of your soul:
You fish with nets of seaweed in the deep   75
As fruitlessly as I with nets of rhyme—
Yet forth you stride, yourself the way, the goal,
The surges are your strides, your path is time.

Hurled by what aim to what tremendous range!
A missile from the great sling of the past,   80
Your passage leaves its track of death and change
And ruin on the world: you fly beyond
Leaping the current of the ages vast
As lightly as a pebble skims a pond.

The years are undulations in your flight   85
Whose awful motion we can only guess—
Too swift for sense, too terrible for sight,
We only know how fast behind you darken
Our days like lonely beacons of distress:
We know that you stride on and will not harken.   90

17

Now in the eastern sky the fairest planet
Pierces the dying wave with dangled spear,
And in the whirring hollows of your granite
That vaster sea to which you are a shell
Sighs with a ghostly rumour, like the drear   95
Moan of the nightwind in a hollow cell.

We shall not meet again; over the wave
Our ways divide, and yours is straight and endless,
But mine is short and crooked to the grave:
Yet what of these dark crowds amid whose flow   100
I battle like a rock, aloof and friendless,
Are not their generations vague and endless
The waves, the strides, the feet on which I go?

[5–14 August 1926. A, SM, CP I]

The Sisters

AFTER hot loveless nights, when cold winds stream
Sprinkling the frost and dew, before the light,
Bored with the foolish things that girls must dream
Because their beds are empty of delight,

Two sisters rise and strip. Out from the night   5
Their horses run to their low-whistled pleas—
Vast phantom shapes with eyeballs rolling white
That sneeze a fiery steam about their knees:

Through the crisp manes their stealthy prowling hands,
Stronger than curbs, in slow caresses rove,   10
They gallop down across the milk-white sands
And wade far out into the sleeping cove:

The frost stings sweetly with a burning kiss
As intimate as love, as cold as death:
Their lips, whereon delicious tremors hiss,   15
Fume with the ghostly pollen of their breath.

Far out on the grey silence of the flood
They watch the dawn in smouldering gyres expand
Beyond them: and the day burns through their blood
Like a white candle through a shuttered hand.   20

[1926. *A, SM, CP* I]

The Zebras

To Chips Rafferty

FROM the dark woods that breathe of fallen showers,
Harnessed with level rays in golden reins,
The zebras draw the dawn across the plains
Wading knee-keep among the scarlet flowers.
The sunlight, zithering their flanks with fire,   5
Flashes between the shadows as they pass
Barred with electric tremors through the grass
Like wind along the gold strings of a lyre.

Into the flushed air snorting rosy plumes
That smoulder round their feet in drifting fumes,   10
With dove-like voices call the distant fillies,
While round the herds the stallion wheels his flight,
Engine of beauty volted with delight,
To roll his mare among the trampled lilies.

[*A, SM, CP* I]

Buffel's Kop

(Olive Schreiner's grave)

IN after times when strength or courage fail,
May I recall this lonely hour: the gloom
Moving one way: all heaven in the gale
Roaring: and high above the insulted tomb
An eagle anchored on full spread of sail   5
That from its wings let fall a silver plume.

[1926. A, CP I]

On Some South African Novelists

YOU praise the firm restraint with which they write—
I'm with you there, of course:
They use the snaffle and the curb all right,
But where's the bloody horse?

[1926. A, CP I]

Selection from *The Wayzgoose**

I

ATTEND my fable if your ears be clean,
In fair Banana Land we lay our scene—
South Africa, renowned both far and wide
For politics and little else beside:

---

* This phenomenon occurs annually in S.A. It appears to be a vast corroboree of journalists, and to judge from their own reports of it, it combines the functions of a bun-fight, an Eisteddfod and an Olympic contest. The Wayzgoose of this poem, however, is not only attended by those who celebrate the function *annually*, but by all the swarms of would-be poets, novelists, philosophers, etc., in South Africa, who should all be compelled to attend such functions *daily*. [RC]

Where, having torn the land with shot and shell,   5
Our sturdy pioneers as farmers dwell,
And, 'twixt the hours of strenuous sleep, relax
To shear the fleeces or to fleece the blacks:
Where every year a fruitful increase bears
Of pumpkins, cattle, sheep, and millionaires—   10
A clime so prosperous both to men and kine
That which were which a sage could scarce define;
Where fat white sheep upon the mountains bleat
And fatter politicians in the street;
Where lemons hang like yellow moons ashine   15
And grapes the size of apples load the vine;
Where apples to the weight of pumpkins go
And donkeys to the height of statesmen grow. . .

    .   .   .   .

Over this rhyme in cafés you will nod,   320
Seem unconcerned when most you feel the rod,
Affect a yawn, pretend a weary smile,
Deplore the taste, and criticize the style.
Yet when at home and by the world unseen,
On senseless paper you will vent your spleen,   325
Claw forth with trembling hand my dainty page
And hurl it on the dustbin in your rage—
In vain you'll strive to hide the blows you catch
And only in my absence, dare to scratch.
For there is one in this most sacred place,   330
English in wit—whatever be my race—
In Durban here—unmentionable brute!—
Who dares the voice of Dullness to refute:
Behold, in naked blasphemy I stalk
And dare to prove I am not made of Pork!   335
Your small horizon, from Berea to Bluff,
Rings you with peace: you may be grim and gruff,
But out beyond—the World will laugh enough!
My words, O Durban, round the World are blown
Where I, alone, of all your sons am known: 340
I circle Tellus with an airy robe—
Thou art the smear I leave upon the globe!

Cobham outsoared, I sail on Satire's wings
Satire, who dares to box the ears of kings,
And comes to statesmen as to roguish boys   345
To snatch from them their baubles and their toys.
In vain you'll strive to minimize my powers
Whose laughter will outlast your tallest towers.
I mock to last: you scold poor rats! to die
Save in my verse where you immortal lie—   350
Yea, when your grandsons bind my works in calf,
Your own unfeeling progeny will laugh
To see their grandsires pickled in my ink—
And Dullness will to future ages stink!

[Begun December 1926, completed 1927. Published 1928,
and in *CP* I]

Rounding the Cape

THE low sun whitens on the flying squalls,
Against the cliffs the long grey surge is rolled
Where Adamastor from his marble halls
Threatens the sons of Lusus as of old.

Faint on the glare uptowers the dauntless form,   5
Into whose shade abysmal as we draw,
Down on our decks, from far above the storm,
Grin the stark ridges of his broken jaw.

Across his back, unheeded, we have broken
Whole forests: heedless of the blood we've spilled,   10
In thunder still his prophecies are spoken,
In silence, by the centuries, fulfilled.

Farewell, terrific shade! though I go free
Still of the powers of darkness art thou Lord:
I watch the phantom sinking in the sea   15
Of all that I have hated or adored.

The prow glides smoothly on through seas quiescent:
But where the last point sinks into the deep,
The land lies dark beneath the rising crescent,
And Night, the Negro, murmurs in his sleep.   20

[1927. *A, SM, CP* I]

Home Thoughts in Bloomsbury

O F all the clever people round me here
I most delight in Me—
Mine is the only voice I care to hear,
And mine the only face I like to see.

[1927. *A, CP* I]

Selection from *The Georgiad*

S o when love's Y.M.W.C.A.,*
Their dinner done, and said their noisy say,
Forming half-sections, with an army's tread,
Along the old oak staircase filed to bed—
Androgyno,† with Georgiana‡ mated,   1405
Into the seventh heaven was translated:
But in his raptures losing all control,
Went far beyond the limits of the soul,
And gave her such a thundering bastinada
As would have sunk the invincible Armada—   1410
Squeals, yells, hysteria, and groans satanic
Through all the house disperse a sort of panic.

* RC's name for Long Barn, the Kent home of Harold Nicolson and his wife Vita
Sackville-West. The Campbell's were the Nicolsons' guests during 1927, and Vita
awakened RC's rage by seducing the poet's wife Mary.
   † RC's powerful bisexual hero.
   ‡ Vita Sackville-West.

And Mr Georgiana* tucks his head
Under his blankets, trembling in his bed,
Thinking some convict's managed to escape   1415
Intent on murder, battery, and rape:
And likewise all the terror-stricken lovers
Who hid like rabbits underneath the covers.
Yet not for long in Georgiana's arms
Our hero lies; but spreading new alarms,   1420
As soon as she collapses, to loud cries,
From bed to bed the amorous fury flies.
The beds, late soothed with homosexual snores,
Began to gallop wildly on the floors;
Like bucking broncos, arching their steel steads, 1425
Those clanking, grim, four-posted quadrupeds
Stampeded, hurdling o'er each others' heads,
As in some wild Grand National of beds.
Like trucks in railway smashes, back to front,
They telescope, rebound, collide, and shunt;   1430
Half Bloomsbury was in that tempest rocked
And some were pleased, but all were truly shocked:
For many a bloodless Fabian learned that night
To his distress, his horror, and affright,
To the destruction of all things genteel   1435
And bloody slaughter of each high ideal,
Far more than any text-book of complexes
Or treatise on the 'meaning of the sexes'
Could have informed him: Freud and Jung and Ellis,
And all the rumblings in the Red Indian bellies, 1440
And all the dark gods that infest our stomachs,
Banshees and bunyips, that perplex and flummox,
That from the unconscience regulate our habits
And in the solar-plexus breed like rabbits,
All these (which it would take ten years to study) 1445
And many other devils wild and bloody
In our Androgyno were then let loose
To put the latest text-books out of use.
Even Mr Georgiana got his share—
They picked him up next morning on the stair   1450
* Harold Nicolson.

24

And brought him to (his nostrils softly shocking)
By holding to his nose a thick blue stocking
Which had belonged (for how long, I forget)
To some old literary suffragette.

Next morning while Androgyno, still tight,   1455
Was sleeping off the efforts of the night,
The indignant boarders all together got
And held a great mass meeting on the spot,
Then telegraphed their horror and distress
To Freud and Jung—an urgent S.O.S.   1460
On the next aeroplane was shipped a yellow
Professor, a most melancholy fellow,
With a great lumping text-book in his fist
And strict instructions (written in a list)
To prove Androgyno did not exist.   1465
Confronted with the culprit, he was ready—
His non-existence had been proved already
Before he'd started, in Freud's own laboratory,
With many freaks of analytic oratory.
So having, on our hero's rank and station,   1470
Even on his rights to clinic tabulation,
And on his title to classification,
Pronounced the ban of excommunication,
With many a hideous howl of execration,
He left by aeroplane, as he had come,   1475
Thinking he'd struck Androgyno quite dumb—
Who for his sermon had not cared a damn,
But having cursed the hostel for a sham,
Punched the hostess, and kicked the poor proprietor,
Went back to London feeling somewhat quieter.   1480
Where now he's editing a posh review—
For solid industry has pulled him through,
Where in the subtle strife of heads or tails
The latter, as by magic, still prevails.

                         [1929. Published 1931 and in *CP* I]

St Peter of the Three Canals

(The Fisher's Prayer)

HIGH in his niche above the town,
The three canals with garbage brown,
The rolling waves, and windy dunes—
An old green idol, thunder-scarred,
On whom the spray has crusted hard,   5
A shell-backed saint, whom time maroons

High stranded on the Rock of Ages,
Of all the ocean-gods and mages
The last surviving Robinson—
Saint Peter-Neptune fronts the wind,   10
In whose Protean rôle combined
All deities and creeds are One.

For when the Three-in-One grow thrifty,
Saint Peter, he is One in Fifty,
Saint Peter, he is All in All!   15
And I have heard the fishers tell
How when from forth the jaws of hell
No other saint would heed their call,

Doomed wretches at the swamping rowlocks
Have seen a saintly Castor-Pollux,   20
Walking the waves, a burning wraith,
Speed to their aid with strides that quicken
As light as Mother Carey's chicken
Foot-webbed with Mercy and with Faith.

Oh, strong is he when winds are strident   25
To tame the water with his trident,
And bold is he when thunders fly,
And swift—outspeeding as he runs
The corposants of Leda's sons—
To heed the sailor's drowning cry.   30

By his high tower of creviced rock
The time is always twelve o'clock—
High tower, high time to save our souls!
And hark! his husky bells are calling
By faith and ivy kept from falling   35
When the night-long mistral rolls.

Deriding Newton, firm and fast,
His crazy tower withstands the blast
A shining miracle to prove—
For all can see, when winds are great,   40
It needs more faith to keep him straight
Than would a range of mountains move.

Around him float on airy sculls
Bright angels in the form of gulls
His seaward messages to go: 45
Deep in his bosom nest the doves
In token of seraphic loves,
To keep his garments—white as snow.

Archbishop of the deep-sea Tritons,
When round his head the glory lightens,   50
Mitred by the moon with flame,
Safe in the harbour that he guards
The masts, adoring, lift their yards
The signal of the cross to frame.

Among the clouds his feet are set,   55
And his hands the spangled net
Where souls of men, as small red fish
Smoked with spindrift, soused in spray, ·
And salted till the Judgement Day,
Await the great Millennial Dish.   60

Amphibious saint, crustacean idol,
At once celestial and tidal,
To his bland creed all doubt atones—
Where Dagon weds with Mother Carey,
Jehovah woos a Mermaid Mary,   65
And Thetis sins with Davey Jones.

Arch-patriarch of Navigation,
He bears the lifebuoy of Salvation
To souls that flounder in the lurch:
With God he walks the azure decks,   70
Great Quartermaster-Pontifex
Whose vessel is the Holy Church.

Her sails are swelled with hymns, her spars
Are pulleyed with the moon and stars
From which depend, a hardy gang,   75
Her crew of human fears and hopes—
And metaphysics are the ropes
By which those desperadoes hang.

Her ropes with love and faith are spliced,
Her compass is the Cross of Christ,   80
Pointing the quarters of the world,
And her auxiliary steam
The vapour of the prophet's dream
To waft her when the winds are furled.

With track of fire she cleaves the distance,   85
To genuflexions of her pistons
The rapture of the turbine rolls:
Her stokehold is the deep Avernus
Where Satan feeds the roaring furnace
And sinners are the burning coals. . . .   90

O Captain of the Saint-filled Ark,
Ere loaded to the Plimsoll mark
Your saintly cargo put to sea,
And we attend the Great Inspection,
The Roll-call of the Resurrection,   95
The pay-day of Eternity—

Remember in your high promotion
How once, poor flotsam of the Ocean,
You followed such a trade as mine.
The winter nights, have you forgotten,   100
When hauling on a seine as rotten
You cracked your knuckles on the line?

Have you forgot the cramp that clinches
Your shoulder, turning at the winches—
And not a mullet in the mesh?   105
Have you forgotten Galilee—
The night you floundered in the sea
Because your faith was in your flesh?

Be with me, then, when nights are lone
And from the pampas of the Rhone,   110
Thrilling with sleet, the great guns blow:
When the black mistral roars avenging
Increase the horse-power of my engine,
Hallow my petrol ere I go!

[Begun 1920, completed late 1929. A, CP I]

Silence

I KNOW your footfall hushed and frail,
Fair siren of the snow-born lake
Whose surface only swans should sail
And only silver hymns should break,
Or thankful prayers devout as this   5
White trophy of a night of sighs
Where Psyche celebrates the kiss
With which a sister closed her eyes.

[A, CP I]

Mass at Dawn

I DROPPED my sail and dried my dripping seines
Where the white quay is chequered by cool planes
In whose great branches, always out of sight,
The nightingales are singing day and night.

Though all was grey beneath the moon's grey beam,   5
My boat in her new paint shone like a bride,
And silver in my baskets shone the bream:
My arms were tired and I was heavy-eyed,
But when with food and drink, at morning-light,
The children met me at the water-side,   10
Never was wine so red or bread so white.

[1929. A, CP I]

Horses on the Camargue*

To A. F. Tschiffely

IN the grey wastes of dread,
The haunt of shattered gulls where nothing moves
But in a shroud of silence like the dead,
I heard a sudden harmony of hooves,
And, turning, saw afar   5
A hundred snowy horses unconfined,
The silver runaways of Neptune's car
Racing, spray-curled, like waves before the wind.
Sons of the Mistral, fleet
As him with whose strong gusts they love to flee,   10
Who shod the flying thunders on their feet
And plumed them with the snortings of the sea;
Theirs is no earthly breed
Who only haunt the verges of the earth
And only on the sea's salt herbage feed—   15
Surely the great white breakers gave them birth.
For when for years a slave,
A horse of the Camargue, in alien lands,
Should catch some far-off fragrance of the wave
Carried far inland from his native sands,   20

* *Camargue*: Pampa at the mouth of the Rhône which together with the Sauvage and the desert Crau form a vast grazing ground for thousands of wild cattle and horses. The Camarguais horses are a distinct race. [RC]

Many have told the tale
Of how in fury, foaming at the rein,
He hurls his rider; and with lifted tail,
With coal-red eyes and cataracting mane,
Heading his course for home,   25
Though sixty foreign leagues before him sweep,
Will never rest until he breathes the foam
And hears the native thunder of the deep.
But when the great gusts rise
And lash their anger on these arid coasts,   30
When the scared gulls career with mournful cries
And whirl across the waste like driven ghosts:
When hail and fire converge,
The only souls to which they strike no pain
Are the white-crested fillies of the surge   35
And the white horses of the windy plain.
Then in their strength and pride
The stallions of the wilderness rejoice;
They feel their Master's trident* in their side,
And high and shrill they answer to his voice.   40
With white tails smoking free,
Long streaming manes, and arching necks, they show
Their kinship to their sisters of the sea—
And forward hurl their thunderbolts of snow.
Still out of hardship bred,   45
Spirits of power and beauty and delight
Have ever on such frugal pastures fed
And loved to course with tempests through the night.

[1929. *A, SM, CP* I]

---

*   *Trident*: dual allusion to the trident of Neptune and that carried by the guardians
or cowboys of the Camargue. [RC]

The Sleeper

SHE lies so still, her only motion
The waves of hair that round her sweep
Revolving to their hushed explosion
Of fragrance on the shores of sleep.
Is it my spirit or her flesh   5
That takes this breathless, silver swoon?
Sleep has no darkness to enmesh
That lonely rival of the moon,
Her beauty, vigilant and white,
That wakeful through the long blue night,   10
Watches, with my own sleepless eyes,
The darkness silver into day,
And through their sockets burns away
The sorrows that have made them wise.

[A, SM, CP I]

The Palm

BLISTERED and dry was the desert I trod
When out of the sky with the step of a god,
Victory-vanned, with her feathers out-fanned,
The palm tree alighting my journey delayed
And spread me, inviting, her carpet of shade.   5
Vain were evasions, though urgent my quest,
And there as the guest of her rustling persuasions
To lie in the shade of her branches was best.
Like a fountain she played, spilling plume over plume in
A leafy cascade for the winds to illumine,   10
Ascending in brilliance and falling in shade,
And spurning the ground with a tiptoe resilience,
Danced to the sound of the music she made.
Her voice intervened on my shadowed seclusion
Like a whispered intrusion of seraph or fiend,   15
In its tone was the hiss of the serpent's wise tongue
But soft as the kiss of a lover it stung—

32

'Unstrung is your lute? For despair are you silent?
Am I not an island in oceans as mute?
Around me the thorns of the desert take root;   20
Though I spring from the rock of a region accurst,
Yet fair is the daughter of hunger and thirst
Who sings like the water the valleys have nursed,
And rings her blue shadow as deep and as cool
As the heavens of azure that sleep on a pool.   25
And you, who so soon by the toil were undone,
Could you guess through what horrors my beauty had won
Ere I crested the noon as the bride of the sun?
The roots are my anchor struck fast in the hill,
The higher I hanker, the deeper they drill,   30
Through the red mortar their claws interlock
To ferret the water through warrens of rock.
Each inch of my glory was wrenched with a groan,
Corroded with fire from the base of my throne
And drawn like a wire from the heart of a stone: 35
Though I soar in the height with a shape of delight
Uplifting my stem like the string of a kite,
Yet still must each grade of my climbing be told
And still from the summit my measure I hold,
Sounding the azure with plummet of gold.   40
Partaking the strain of the heavenward pride
That soars me away from the earth I deride,
Though my stem be a rein that would tether me down
And fasten a chain on the height of my crown,
Yet through its tense nerve do I measure my might,   45
The strain of its curb is the strength of my flight:
And when, by the hate of the hurricane blown,
It doubles its forces with fibres that groan,
Exulting I ride in the tower of my pride
To feel that the strength of the blast is my own . . .   50
Rest under my branches, breathe deep of my balm
From the hushed avalanches of fragrance and calm,
For suave is the silence that poises the palm.
The wings of the egrets are silken and fine,
But hushed with the secrets of Eden are mine: 55
Your spirit that grieves like the wind in my leaves
Shall be robbed of its care by those whispering thieves

To study my patience and hear, the day long,
The soft foliations of sand into song—
For bitter and cold though it rasp to my root,   60
Each atom of gold is the chance of a fruit,
The sap is the music, the stem is the flute,
And the leaves are the wings of the seraph I shape
Who dances, who springs in a golden escape,
Out of the dust and the drought of the plain,   65
To sing with the silver hosannas of rain.'

[A, SM, CP I]

Estocade

A CLUMSY bull, obscene and fat,
Who wears the devil's pointed hat
And cloven shoe,
Seems from my brain a sylph to call
To tease him with my flaming shawl   5
And thrust his shoulders through.

Dull eyes, like owls', that shrink away
Insulted from the light of day
In bloodshot gloom,
In my red silk see only night   10
And in my flame of steel no light
To glorify their doom—

No more can this blind passion claim,
Across whose blurred instinctive aim
My cape I swung,   15
Into a tumbled heap diverting
Its steel-shot bulk with redly-squirting
Nose and lolling tongue.

For though to frenzy still be stirred
The unwieldy lecher of the herd,   20
Still to its brain
I am all wings and airy lightness
And make a comet of my whiteness
In that black sky of pain.

[*A, SM, CP* I]

Autumn

I LOVE to see, when leaves depart,
The clear anatomy arrive,
Winter, the paragon of art,
That kills all forms of life and feeling
Save what is pure and will survive.   5

Already now the clanging chains
Of geese are harnessed to the moon:
Stripped are the great sun-clouding planes:
And the dark pines, their own revealing,
Let in the needles of the noon.   10

Strained by the gale the olives whiten
Like hoary wrestlers bent with toil
And, with the vines, their branches lighten
To brim our vats where summer lingers
In the red froth and sun-gold oil.   15

Soon on our hearth's reviving pyre
Their rotted stems will crumble up:
And like a ruby, panting fire,
The grape will redden on your fingers
Through the lit crystal of the cup.   20

[Late 1929. *A, SM, CP* I]

35

The Gum Trees

To Alister Kershaw

HALF-HID by leaves, in lofty shoots,
The long lit files of stems arise,
An orchestra of silver flutes
That sing with movement to the eyes:

A movement born of rustling sound,   5
A rapid stillness, anchored flight,
That far along the level ground
Carries the distance out of sight.

Each interval between their feet
A dryad's stride, as they recede   10
In immobility more fleet
Than in the whizzing wind of speed,

Far on the sky, with crests aflame,
The tapering avenues unite,
And to a single target aim   15
The keen velocities of sight;

They snare the eye with clues of speed,
And with the wandering gaze elope:
The sight must follow where they lead,
As running water does the slope;   20

The impetus their beauty breeds
Is like a silver current hurled
Majestic through the noiseless reeds
Of some less transitory world;

Out of the bounds at which we stick   25
To what dimensions are they freed
By such superb arithmetic
To multiply their strength and speed?

Along the red-lit rim of space
In lofty cadences they rhyme,   30
Their march is one victorious race
Of immobility with time;

Far down each rapid colonnade
Their paces cut the shadows white,
They step across their pools of shade   35
With intervals of silver light;

In shuttered ranks across the gale
They flicker to the moon's white fire,
Like sleepers to an airy rail
They rush beneath her golden tyre;   40

Softly as a breeze that slumbers
They glide across the tufted floor,
For their motion is in numbers
And the shadows are their spoor.

They are the footfalls of the light,   45
Slippered with rustling leaves they run
Across the darkness of the night
To fetch the white blaze of the sun;

But as the gloom around them fades,
The old hallucination flees,   50
They swiften through the rushing shades
Their endless marathon of trees;

The winds they wrestled with are thrown,
The miles they trekked are spurned and dead,
But there before the blazing throne   55
They blacken into shapes of dread,

And on and on without control
Still in the same direction tread:
They, too, have dreamed they sought a goal
When merely from themselves they fled!   60

Their giant skeletons of shade
Are blackly charred upon the eye,
In motley rags of gloom arrayed
They wear the scorn of earth and sky.

The dusty winds begin to sweep,   65
The distance stretched before them lies,
Antaeus-like from caves of sleep
Their old antagonists arise.

                              [1929. *FR, CP* I]

Canaan

BENEATH us stream the golden hours
The slower for our hearts, where now,
Two ripe grenades on the same bough,
Their globes of bronze together swung,
Have stayed the stream they overhung   5
With fallen heaps of flowers.

For never was she half so fair
Whose colours bleed the red rose white
And milk the lilies of their light:
In her snowed breasts where sorrow dies,   10
All the white rills of Canaan rise,
And cedars in her hair.

Half-way across a flowery land
Through which our still reluctant feet
Must pass, for every halt too fleet,   15
We pause upon the topmost hill
Whence streams of wine and honey spill
To some rapacious strand.

38

There, sisters of the milky way,
The rills of Canaan sing and shine: 20
Diluvial in the waves of wine
Whose gulls are rosy-footed doves
The glorious bodies of my loves
Like dolphins heave the spray—

Red Rhones towards the sounding shore   25
Through castled gorges roaring down
By many a tiered and towery town,
High swollen with a spate of hours,
And strewn with all the dying flowers
That we shall love no more—   30

Torrential in the nightingale,
My spirit hymns them as they go
For wider yet their streams must flow
With flowery trophies heaped more high
Before they drain their sources dry   35
And those clear fountains fail.

I cannot think (so blue the day)
That those fair castalies of dreams
Or the cool naiads of their streams,
Or I, the willow in whose shade   40
Their wandering music was delayed,
Should pass like ghosts away.

The azure triumphs on the height:
Life is sustained with golden arms:
The fire-red cock with loud alarms   45
Arising, drums his golden wings
And in the victory he sings,
The Sun insults the night.

O flying hair and limbs of fire
Through whose frail forms, that fade and pass,   50
Tornadoing as flame through grass,
Eternal beauty flares alone
To build herself a blazing throne
Out of the world's desire—

The summer leaves are whirled away: 55
The fallen chestnut in the grass
Is trampled by the feet that pass
And like the young Madonna's heart
With rosy portals gashed apart
Bleeds for the things I say.   60

[FR, CP I]

Song

YOU ask what far-off singing
Has mingled with our rest.
It is my love that, winging
The deep wave of your breast,
With white sail homeward turning,   5
Sings at the golden oar
Of a white city burning
On the battle-tented shore.

[FR, CP I]

Autumn Plane

PEELED white and washed with fallen rain,
A dancer weighed with jingling pearls,
The girl-white body of a plane,
In whose red hair the Autumn swirls,
Stands out, soliciting the cruel   5
Flame of the wintry sun, and dies,
If only to the watcher's eyes,
In red-gold anguish glowing; fuel
To that cold fire, as she assumes
(Brunhilde) her refulgent plumes   10
In leaves that kindle as they die,
Of all that triumphs and returns   ·
The furious aurora burns
Against the winter-boding sky.

[FR, CP I]

The Flame

In the blue darkness of your hair,
Smouldering on from birth to death,
My love is like the burnish there
That I can kindle with a breath.
Or like the flame in this black wine   5
Upon whose raven wings we rise
Lighter in spirit than the sighs
With which the purple roses twine:
Like a great star with steady beam
It runs against a darkened stream,   10
And from its onrush of despairs
Draws all the splendours of my blood,
As I have seen the Rhone in flood
Drawn starward by the golden hairs.

[FR, CP I]

The Blue Wave

The blue wave resembles
The moment we hold
By its tresses of gold,
For it flushes and trembles,
And is drawn by the fiery   5
Low sun from the sea
Where his sister and he,
Sailing home to their eyrie
Like eagles to nest,
Bear it on like the hour   10
That we hold in our power,
When the day like a dragon
Has sunken its crest,
And the star in our flagon
Is that in the West.   15

[FR, CP I]

41

Wings

WHEN gathering vapours climb in storm
The steep sierras of delight,
Wings of your hair I love to form
And on its perfume soar from sight.
For in those great black plumes unfurled   5
The darkest condor of my thought
May stretch his aching sinews taut
And fling his shadow on the world.
When sick of self my moods rebel,
The demon from his secret hell,   10
The eagle from his cage of brass,
They have been lent such scented wings
Over the wreck of earthly things
In silence with the sun to pass.

[FR, CP I]

Swans

THE dark trees slept, none to the azure true,
Save where alone, the glory of the glade,
The cone of one tall cypress cut the blue
And azure on the marble dreamed its shade:
As long as I could feel it next to mine   5
Her body was illumined by my ghost,
As through the silver of the lighted host
Might flush the ruby reflex of the wine.
The night ran like a river deep and blue:
The reeds of thought, with humming silver wands, 10
Brushed by our silence like a fleet of swans,
Sang to the passing wave their faint adieu.
Stars in that current quenched their dying flame
Like folding flowers: till down the silent streams,
Swan-drawn among the lilies, slumber came,   15
Veiling with rosy hand the lamp of dreams.

[FR, CP I]

Choosing a Mast

THIS mast, new-shaved, through whom I rive the ropes,
Says she was once an oread of the slopes,
Graceful and tall upon the rocky highlands,
A slender tree as vertical as noon,
And her low voice was lovely as the silence   5
Through which a fountain whistles to the moon,
Who now of the white spray must take the veil
And, for her songs, the thunder of the sail.

I chose her for her fragrance, when the spring
With sweetest resins swelled her fourteenth ring   10
And with live amber welded her young thews:
I chose her for the glory of the Muse,
Smoother of forms, that her hard-knotted grain,
Grazed by the chisel, shaven by the plane,
Might from the steel as cool a burnish take   15
As from the bladed moon a windless lake.

I chose her for her eagerness of flight
Where she stood tiptoe on the rocky height
Lifted by her own perfume to the sun,
While through her rustling plumes with eager sound   20
Her eagle spirit, with the gale at one,
Spreading wide pinions, would have spurned the ground
And her own sleeping shadow, had they not
With thymy fragrance charmed her to the spot.

Lover of song, I chose this mountain pine   25
Not only for the straightness of her spine
But for her songs: for there she loved to sing
Through a long noon's repose of wave and wing,
The fluvial swirling of her scented hair
Sole rill of song in all that windless air,   30
And her slim form the naiad of the stream
Afloat upon the languor of its theme;

And for the soldier's fare on which she fed:
Her wine the azure, and the snow her bread;
And for her stormy watches on the height,   35
For only out of solitude or strife
Are born the sons of valour and delight;
And lastly for her rich, exulting life,
That with the wind stopped not its singing breath
But carolled on, the louder for its death.   40

Under a pine, when summer days were deep,
We loved the most to lie in love or sleep:
And when in long hexameters the west
Rolled his grey surge, the forest for his lyre,
It was the pines that sang us to our rest,   45
Loud in the wind and fragrant in the fire,
With legioned voices swelling all night long,
From Pelion to Provence, their storm of song.

It was the pines that fanned us in the heat,
The pines, that cheered us in the time of sleet,   50
For which sweet gifts I set one dryad free;
No longer to the wind a rooted foe,
This nymph shall wander where she longs to be
And with the blue north wind arise and go,
A silver huntress with the moon to run   55
And fly through rainbows with the rising sun;

And when to pasture in the glittering shoals
The guardian mistral drives his thundering foals,
And when like Tartar horsemen racing free
We ride the snorting fillies of the sea,   60
My pine shall be the archer of the gale
While on the bending willow curves the sail
From whose great bow the long keel shooting home
Shall fly, the feathered arrow of the foam.

[April 1931. *FR, CP* I]

The Secret Muse

BETWEEN the midnight and the morn,
To share my watches late and lonely,
There dawns a presence such as only
Of perfect silence can be born.
On the blank parchment falls the glow   5
Of more than daybreak: and one regal
Thought, like the shadow of an eagle,
Grazes the smoothness of its snow.
Though veiled to me that face of faces
And still that form eludes my art,   10
Yet all the gifts my faith has brought
Along the secret stair of thought
Have come to me on those hushed paces
Whose footfall is my beating heart.

[P, FR, CP I]

The Rejoneador

WHILE in your lightly veering course
A seraph seems to take his flight,
The swervings of your snowy horse,
Volted with valour and delight,
In thundering orbit wheel the Ring   5
Which Apis pivots with his pain
And of whose realm, with royal stain,
His agony anoints you king.
His horns the moon, his hue the night,
The dying embers of his sight   10
Across their bloody film may view
The star of morning rise in fire,
Projectile of the same desire
Whose pride is animate in you.

[P, FR, CP I]

La Clemence*

WHEN with white wings and rhyme of rapid oars
The sisters of your speed, as fleet as you,
With silver scythes, the reapers of the blue,
Turn from their harvest to the sunset shores;

When the pine-heaving mistral rolls afar   5
The sounding gust that your stiff pinion loves,
And rose-lit sails, a thousand homing doves
With foamy ribbons draw the wave-born Star;

May you be first her rising torch to greet
And first within the distant port to ride,   10
Your triangle of silver for her guide,
Your pearling prow a sandal to her feet.

[P, FR, CP I]

* 'La Clemence' was the name of a boat Campbell owned when he lived in Martigues.

Reflection

MY thought has learned the lucid art
By which the willows lave their limbs,
Whose form upon the water swims
Though in the air they rise apart.
For when with my delight I lie,   5
By purest reason unreproved,
Psyche usurps the outward eye
To trace her inward sculpture grooved
In one melodious line, whose flow
With eddying circle now invests   10
The rippled silver of her breasts,
Now shaves a flank of rose-lit snow,
Or rounds a cheek where sunset dies
In the black starlight of her eyes.

[P, FR, CP I]

The Olive Tree I

In a bare country shorn of leaf,
By no remote sierra screened,
Where pauses in the wind are brief
As the remorses of a fiend,
The stark Laocoon this tree   5
Forms of its knotted arm and thigh
In snaky tussle with a sky
Whose hatred is eternity,
Through his white fronds that whirl and seethe
And in the groaning root he screws,   10
Makes heard the cry of all who breathe,
Repulsing and accusing still
The Enemy who shaped his thews
And is inherent to his will.

                                    [*P, FR, CP* I]

The Olive Tree II

Curbed athlete hopeless of the palm,
If in the rising moon he hold,
Discobolos, a quoit of gold
Caught in his gusty sweep of arm,
Or if he loom against the dawn,   5
The circle where he takes his run
To hurl the discus of the sun
Is by his own dark shadow drawn:
The strict arena of his game
Whose endless effort is denied   10
More room for victory or pride
Than what he covers with his shame.

                                    [*P, FR, CP* I]

47

A Sleeping Woman

REDDENING through the gems of frost
That twinkle on the milk-white thorn,
Softly hesitates the morn
In whom as yet no star is lost.
From skies the colour of her skin,   5
So touched with golden down, so fair,
Where glittering cypress seems to spin
The black refulgence of her hair,
Clear as a glass the day replies
To every feature save her eyes   10
But shows their lashes long and fine
Across her cheek by slumber drawn,
As the black needles of the pine
Are feathered on the flush of dawn.

[P, FR, CP I]

Overtime

To Peter Eaton

AMONGST the ponderous tomes of learning,
Dull texts of medicine and law,
With idle thumb the pages turning
In sudden carnival, I saw,
Revelling forth into the day   5
In scarlet liveries, nine or ten
Survivors of their own decay—
The flayed anatomies of men:
And marked how well the scalpel's care
Was aided by the painter's tones   10
To liven with a jaunty air
Their crazy trellises of bones.
In regimental stripes and bands
Each emphasized the cause he serves—
Here was a grenadier of glands   15
And there a gay hussar of nerves:

48

And one his skin peeled off, as though
A workman's coat, with surly shrug
The flexion of the thews to show,
Treading a shovel, grimly dug.   20
Dour sexton, working overtime,
With gristly toes he hooked his spade
To trench the very marl and slime
In which he should have long been laid.
The lucky many of the dead—   25
Their suit of darkness fits them tight,
Buttoned with stars from foot to head
They wear the uniform of Night;
But some for extra shift are due
Who, slaves for any fool to blame,   30
With a flayed sole the ages through
Must push the shovel of their fame.

[FR, CP I]

The Road to Arles

FROM the cold huntress shorn of any veil
Bare trees, the target of her silver spite,
Down the long avenue in staggy flight
Are hunted by the hungers of the gale:
Along the cold grey torrent of the sky   5
Where branch the fatal trophies of his brows,
Actaeon, antlered in the wintry boughs,
Rears to the stars his mastiff-throttled cry.
Pride has avenging arrows for the eyes
That strip her beauty silver of disguise,   10
And she has dogs before whose pace to flee—
In front a waste, behind a bended bow,
And a long race across the stony Crau
Torn in each gust, and slain in every tree.

[1933. FR, CP I]

The Hat

BENEATH our feet we heard the soaring larks;
The sunlight had the hum of winnowed chaff,
And the blue wind was sown with tingling sparks,
That blew my hat away to make you laugh.
Over the land it sailed, collected height,   5
Flapped in the face of each offended crow,
And scared the speckled falcon of the Baux,
Adventurously taunting it to fight.
Like Saturn's in its whirling shady brim,
Far down, its giant shadow coursed the plain—   10
Never did autogyre so lively skim
As did the flying discus of my brain;
And though my skull, a mile or so behind,
Left to the cold phrenologizing wind,
Shone bald and egg-like in the noonday sun—   15
This fantasy was left to hatch alone,
A sudden brainwave, breaching through the bone,
That for a breathless minute made us one
With that unsated wish in us, that lives
Out of this merely positive degree   20
In the wide region of superlatives,
Translating every rash hyperbole
We utter, into life and action there;
Out of our foibles founding pyramids;
And friezing dizzy Parthenons of air   25
With deeds that our heredity forbids.

[*ME, CP* I]

The Solar Enemy

ENEMY of my inward night
and victor of its bestial Signs
whose arm against the Bull designs
the red veronicas of light:
your cape a roaring gale of gold   5
in furious auroras swirled,
the scarlet of its outward fold
is of a dawn beyond the world—
a sky of intellectual fire
through which the stricken beast may view   10
its final agony aspire
to sun the broad aeolian blue—
my own lit heart, its rays of fire,
the seven swords that run it through.

[1933. *ME, CP* I]

The Seven Swords

OF seven hues in white elision,*
the radii of your silver gyre,
are the seven swords of vision
that spoked the prophets' flaming tyre;
their sistered stridences ignite   5
the spectrum of the poets' lyre
whose unison becomes a white
revolving disc of stainless fire,
and sights the eye of that sole star
that, in the heavy clods we are,   10
the kindred seeds of fire can spy,
or, in the cold shell of the rock,
the red yolk of the phoenix-cock
whose feathers in the meteors fly.

[1933. *ME, CP* I]

* The seven colours of the rainbow when painted on a swiftly revolving disc
combine to form the purest whiteness. [RC]

The First Sword

THE first's of lunar crystal hewn,
a woman's beauty, through whose snows
the volted ecstasy outglows
a dolphin dying in the noon;
and fights for love, as that for life,   5
and leaps and turns upon its side
and swirls the anger of its strife
a radiant iris far and wide,
bronze, azure, and auroral rose
faint-flushing through its nacreous snows—   10
electric in a god's strong hand
this sword was tempered in my blood
when all its tides were at the flood
and heroes fought upon the strand.

[Early 1933. ME, CP I]

The Second Sword

CLEAR spirits of the waveless sea
have steeped the second in their light,
a low blue flame, the halcyon's flight
passing at sunset swift and free
along the miles of tunny-floats   5
when the soft swell in slumber rolls
and sways the lanterns on their poles
and idly rocks the drifting boats;
when evening strews the rosy fleece
and the low conches sound from far,   10
a lonely bird whose sword of air
is hilted with the evening star
has slain upon the shrine of peace
the daily slaving forms I wear.

[Early 1933. ME, CP I]

The Third Sword

LIKE moonbeams on a wintry sea
the third is sorrowful and pale
and from my vision guards the grail
whose glory I shall never see;
a boreal streamer burning green,   5
it shivers in a land of shade
as if some wandering Cain had seen
his soul reflected in its blade.
It glitters in some frozen hold
that leaves its icy hilt unthawn;   10
its radius is a flame of cold,
the skyline of an arctic dawn;
Vulcan in forging it grew old
and sorrow froze when it was drawn.

[1933. *ME, CP* I]

The Fourth Sword

IN crimson sash and golden vest
a gay daedalion of the day
transfixing with a sworded ray
its black and melancholy breast,
the tiger-fly with whirring vans   5
rifles a sombre grape, whose heart,
red-glowing to the hilted dart,
seems a lit furnace that he fans—
so to the soured and black despairs
my blasted vine in autumn bears,   10
so horneted with strident wings,
to his own trumpet peal and drum
the toreadoring sylph will come
and anger is the sword he brings.

[Early 1933. *ME, CP* I]

The Fifth Sword

SILENT and vertical and dim
the lunar flambeau of a prayer
that rising in the frosty air
is silvered by the seraphim,
thawing the night with airy blade,   5
like a funereal candle set
to burn the fuel of regret
(though in the noon it casts a shade)
the fifth, a lifetime to consume,
in vigilance is still the same,   10
a sword of silver in the gloom
it guards a grief that is my shame;
by day a cypress on a tomb,
but in the night it is a flame.

[1933. *ME, CP* I]

The Sixth Sword

FROM that Toledo of the brain
where none but perfect steel is wrought,
of all its cities thronged with thought
that soars the farthest from the plain,
clear lightning with a sheath of gold,   5
a scarlet tassel at the hilt,
a blade the noonday sun to jilt
and sparkle in a cherub's hold,
the sixth salutes the last Crusade
and her, by all the world betrayed,   10
who reared its red and golden streamer
upon the ramparts of Castile—
of the great West the sole redeemer
and rainbow of the Storms of Steel.

[July 1933; recast 1948. *ME, CP* I]

The Seventh Sword

THE seventh arms a god's desire
who lusts, in Psyche, to possess
his white reluctant pythoness;
as in the fugitive of fire,
pale ice, the sworded flame is caught;   5
or the red images of ire
in the pure person of a thought.
As arctic crystals that would shun,
but each become, the living sun,
where best his image may be sought;   10
so to the shining sword he probes,
her breasts are lighted, and their globes
each to a vase of crystal wrought.

[1933. *ME, CP* I]

The Raven II

UPON the red crag of my heart
his gorgeous pinions came to rest
where year by year with curious art
he piles the faggots of his nest,
old forest antlers lichen-hoary   5
and driftwood fished from lunar seas
that once had blossomed with the lory
and trumpeted the golden bees:
and steeper yet he stacks the pyre
to tempt the forked, cremating fire   10
to strike, to kindle, and consume:
till answering beacons shall attest
that fire is in the Raven's nest
and resurrection in the tomb.

[1934. *ME, CP* I]

Death of the Bull

THOSE horns, the envy of the moon,
now, targeting the sun, have set:
the eyes are cinders of regret
that were the tinder of the noon.
But from the hornèd Alp that kneels,   5
as if the Rhône should sluice its flood,
out of a Wound that never heals
rills forth the lily-scented blood,
the snow-fed wine of scarlet stain,
that widens, flowering through the plains,   10
and from the Wound its anguish drains—
as you may hear from one who drank,
down on his knees, beside the bank,
and lost the memory of pain.

[June 1936. ME, CP I]

The Morning

THE woods have caught the singing flame
in live bouquets of loveliest hue—
the scarlet fink, the chook, the sprew,
that seem to call me by my name.
Such friendship, understanding, truth,   5
this morning from its Master took
as if San Juan de la Cruz
had written it in his own book,
and went on reading it aloud
until his voice was half the awe   10
with which this loneliness is loud,
and every word were what I saw
live, shine, or suffer in that Ray
whose only shadow is our day.

[ME, CP I]

56

To the Sun*

OH let your shining orb grow dim,
Of Christ the mirror and the shield,
That I may gaze through you to Him,
See half the miracle revealed,
And in your seven hues behold   5
The Blue Man walking on the Sea;
The Green, beneath the summer tree,
Who called the children; then the Gold,
With palms; the Orange, flaring bold
With scourges; Purple in the garden   10
(As Greco saw): and then the Red
Torero (Him who took the toss
And rode the black horns of the cross—
But rose snow-silver from the dead!)

[*ME, CP* I]

Creeping Jesus†

PALE crafty eyes beneath his ginger crop,
A fox's snout with spectacles on top—
Eye to the keyhole, kneeling on the stair,
We often found this latter saint at prayer,
'For your own sake,' he'd tell you with a sigh   5
(He always did his kindness on the sly).
He paid mere friendship with his good advice
And swarmed with counsels as a cur with lice:
For his friends' actions, with unerring snout,
He'd always fox his own low motives out,   10
And having found them, trot them out to view,
Saying it hurt him so much more than you!
Sober, astute, and modest in his mien,
Between extremes he always chose the *mean*,
For Epsom mounted quickly to his head   15
And he saw brown where other men saw red.

* This was the last poem of Mithraic Emblems, but I judged it better to separate
it. [RC]
† An attack on William Plomer.

57

Walking Locarno between friend and friend
He soured the quarrels he so loved to mend.
In him the 'friend' concealed the jealous 'tante'
Who slandered women he could not supplant,   20
Whose faults he would invent and then reveal
On the pretext of trying to conceal.
He'd blurt a secret (none so sure as he)
By hiding it so hard that all could see.
He'd make men black in everybody's eye—   25
Taking their part, so stoutly to deny
Things they had never done, nor none suspected . . .
Until his stout defence was interjected!
No dun with more reluctance or regret
Ever came knocking to present a debt,   30
Than he so mildly, sadly would reproach
A friend—or any painful subject broach.
His martyred look no mortal could resist
More than a gossamer to Dempsey's fist,
It had the power to put you in the wrong   35
And suck excuses from a rawhide thong.
When of apologies your heart was poor
You always seemed to owe him more and more,
The star of Tartuffe by his own grew dim
And Pecksniff was a nincompoop to him!   40
He was the guy to censure or expunge
The folk on whom he'd condescend to sponge,
And when he ate you out of hearth and home,
On independence lecture you a tome.
A counter-jumper born of base degree   45
In all the world no greater snob than he,
Though he descended from some anglo-parson
Who had committed [something else than] arson,
And looked it—had you made his collar shunt
To tally with its owner, *back-to-front!*   50
So satisfied his smirk, so smug his snigger,
You'd take him for a deacon or a vicar;
His pale blue smile was full of deany dope
And in his hand a cake of Monkey Soap.
If we put up with him—'twas as a bug   55
In his own talent (an expensive rug),

58

But he abused its lovely silken floss,
One tiny insect spoiled the whole kaross:
The leather's perished, moulted all the hair,
But the old bug is still established there!   60

[1933. *ME, CP* I]

The Dead Torero

SUCH work can be the mischief of an hour.
This drunken-looking doll without a face
Was lovely Florentino. This was grace
And virtue smiling on the face of Power.

Shattered, that slim Toledo-tempered spine!   5
Hollow, the chrysalis, his gentle hand,
From which those wide imperial moths were fanned
Each in its hushed miraculous design!

He was the bee, with danger for his rose!
He died the sudden violence of Kings,   10
And from the bullring to the Virgin goes
Floating his cape. He has no need for wings.

[May 1934. *ME* (as 'Florentino Ballesteros II'), *CP* I]

The Fight

ONE silver-white and one of scarlet hue,
Storm-hornets humming in the wind of death,
Two aeroplanes were fighting in the blue
Above our town; and if I held my breath,
It was because my youth was in the Red   5
While in the White an unknown pilot flew—
And that the White had risen overhead.

59

From time to time the crackle of a gun
Far into flawless ether faintly railed,
And now, mosquito-thin, into the Sun,   10
And now like mating dragonflies they sailed:
And, when like eagles near the earth they drove,
The Red, still losing what the White had won,
The harder for each lost advantage strove.

So lovely lay the land—the towers and trees   15
Taking the seaward counsel of the stream:
The city seemed, above the far-off seas,
The crest and turret of a Jacob's dream,
And those two gun-birds in their frantic spire
At death-grips for its ultimate regime—   20
Less to be whirled by anger than desire.

Till (Glory!) from his chrysalis of steel
The Red flung wide the fatal fans of fire:
I saw the long flames, ribboning, unreel,
And slow bitumen trawling from his pyre.   25
I knew the ecstasy, the fearful throes,
And the white phoenix from his scarlet sire,
As silver in the Solitude he rose.

The towers and trees were lifted hymns of praise,
The city was a prayer, the land a nun: 30
The noonday azure strumming all its rays
Sang that a famous battle had been won,
As signing his white Cross, the very Sun,
The Solar Christ and captain of my days
Zoomed to the zenith; and his will was done.   35

[1934. ME, CP I]

A Jug of Water

To Armand Guibert

THE snow-born sylph, her spools of glory spun,
Forgets the singing journeys that she came
To fill this frosty chrysalis of flame
Where sleeps a golden echo of the Sun.

The silver life and swordplay of the noon   5
Caught in mid-slash; the wildfire of the scar
Whose suds of thunder in a crystal jar
Compose a silent image of the moon.

Shut rainbow; hushed appeasement of the spray;
Meeting of myriad dews, as if to show   10
Aurora's hand from out whose cup of snow
The solar horses drink the fires of day.

A masquer so anonymously white
Who smiles without a face: a cloister frail
In whose clear precinct music takes the veil   15
And sings, but to the vision, with its light;—

It was the psalm and incense of the plain,
The sleep-heard music humming on the roofs,
The candle lighted by our horses' hoofs
When we rode home by moonlight after rain.   20

When tinder to a star it lay at night
Holding it like a glow-worm in its hand;
Or in a shallow ripple shaved the sand
Filming a stormy shipwreck of the light—

Still was its only study to acquire   25
Embryon ecstasies, the sperm of power—
Rose of the dawn, or nimbus of the shower
To sail, a ship of love, on seas of fire.

Its luck was always to sustain a King,
The jingled spur and stirrup of the cloud—   30
To launch a swan by the same art endowed
Or smooth the pebbles for a David's sling.

True phoenix-fuel whom no burning mars
But pain and fire resuscitate afresh,
It has put on all forms of flame or flesh   35
And trawled the lovely bodies of the stars.

And once it was a youth before he died
To form this lily-calyx for the light,
Who made a pond his palace of delight
And thought himself beside the sun enskied.   40

With stars and flying clouds about him rolled
High in that silver paradise ensphered,
Down from his gaze his fatal beauty sheered,
A marble precipice, with ferns of gold.

Echo his dirge, the zephyr is his shroud,   45
Whose pride with running water was but one:
And both a brief reflection of the sun
Which any sigh suffices for a cloud.

Though every passing yearner for the skies
Out of his glass construct a secret hell,   50
If with our own reflections we must dwell
Let them be seen in one another's eyes.

This crystal by a different hand is wheeled,
And here the sun its circle seems to dim
That we may see undazzled through to Him   55
Of whom it is the mirror or the shield.

Stagnant in drains where beauty scorns to bathe,
Yet who has seen it unalloyed with Light
Has seen black snow, has seen unanswered faith,
And courage unrewarded with delight.   60

Pool in the grime by city lanterns scarred
Stainless it still from every contact came
As the light incense, orphan of the flame,
Survives the baser fuel it has charred.

Sight of the Earth, for every star an eye,   65
The element by which it sees and thinks,
It signs upon that stark and rocky Sphinx
Her smile of resignation to the sky.

Here though in exile from the singing shower,
It seems to boast its quiet faith—'To me   70
The world is like a trogon-feathered tree
That never sheds its leaves except to flower.'

It says it is the blossom in our blood
With folded petals smiling out the sere,
Brown, shuffled slippers of the limping year—   75
The leaves that drift and whisper in the mud.

Complain those burned brown leaves? then let them go!
(Though who should whimper whom the sun has kissed?)
That flowers may come, outsilvering the mist,
To stain the boasted ermines of the snow.   80

And now the world's great autumn blows at last,
The brown horde yells before it, questing death—
Folding its cape, this waits with baited breath
To flaunt its cool evasion of the blast.

White armour of the world's exultant strife,   85
In it the sunbeam is a lance at rest:
And like a sword the lightning in its breast
Lies hidden, with the miracle of life.

Wings, flowers, and flames are folded in its peace—
This common water where the sunlight falls;   90
Shake it, and from your hand you can release
A flight of coloured pigeons round the walls.

Rest, twinkling valour! on my friendly sill
When sheep are rabid, serpents well may rest.
(Coil, Christian Tagus, round the sacred hill,   95
That wears the steep Alcazar for a crest!)

But when your great commandos, in the rain
Shall gallop singing on our thirsty lands,
Down on my knees, my hat between my hands,
I'll drink the huge elation of the plain.   100

Your spirit sings (and to its sister sprite)
That love is God, that dying is renewal,
That we are flames, and the black world is fuel
To hearts that burn and battle for delight.

[1934. *ME, CP* I]

Dedication of a Tree

To 'Peter Warlock'

THIS laurel-tree to Heseltine* I vow
With one cicada silvering its shade—
Who lived, like him, a golden gasconade,
And will die whole when winter burns the bough:
Who in one hour, resounding, clear, and strong,   5
A century of ant-hood far out-glows,
And burns more sunlight in a single song
Than they can store against the winter snows.

[*ME, CP* I]

* The composer Philip Heseltine, a close friend of Campbell's in the late 1920s,
used the pen-name 'Peter Warlock'.

Posada

OUTSIDE, it froze. On rocky arms
Sleeping face-upwards to the sun
Lay Spain. Her golden hair was spun
From sky to sky. Her mighty charms
Breathed soft beneath her robe of farms   5
And gardens: while her snowy breasts,
Sierras white, with crimson crests,
Were stained with sunset. At the Inn,
A priest, a soldier, and a poet
(Fate-summoned, though they didn't know it)   10
Met there, a shining hour to win.
A song, a blessing, and a grin
Were melted in one cup of mirth,
The Eternal Triumvirs of Earth
Foresaw their golden age begin.   15

[1935. *ME, CP* I]

After the Horse-fair

A MULE, the snowball of a beast!
(Ring out the duros, test the tune)
And a guitar, the midnight lark,
That rises silvering the dark
An hour before the rosy-fleeced   5
Arrival of the Moon.

The gypsies quarried from the gloom,
For their carouse, a silver hall:
And jingled harness filled the lands
With gay pesetas changing hands,   10
So silvery, there seemed no room
For any moon at all.

Two figtrees on a whitewashed wall
Were playing chess; a lamp was queen:
Beneath the civil guard were seen   15
With tricorned hats—a game of cards:
One bottle was between them all,
Good health, and kind regards.

A stable with an open door
And in the yard a dying hound: 20
Out on the dunes a broken spoor
Converging into twenty more—
When torches had been flashed around
Was all they could restore.

A wind that blows from other countries   25
Shook opals from the vernal palms
Birdshot of the silver huntress
By which the nightingale was slain:
With stitch of fire the distant farms
Were threaded by the train.   30

One rider, then, and all alone—
The long Castilian Veld before:
To show the way his shadow straight
Went on ahead and would not wait,
But seemed, so infinitely grown,   35
Equator to the moor.

Till with a faint adoring thunder,
Their lances raised to Christ the King,
Through all the leagues he had to go—
An army chanting smooth and low,   40
Across the long mirage of wonder
He heard the steeples sing.

And as, far off, the breaking morn
Had hit the high seraphic town,
He prayed for lonesome carbineers   45
And wakeful lovers, rash of years,
Who've harvested the lunar corn
Before the crops were brown.

For thieves: the gate-man late and lonely
With his green flag; for tramps that sprawl: 50
And lastly for a frozen guy
That towed six mules along the sky
And felt among them all the only,
Or most a mule of all!

[1935. *ME, CP* I]

Driving Cattle to Casas Buenas

THE roller perched upon the wire,
Telegrams running through his toes,
At my approach would not retire
But croaked a greeting as he rose,
A telegraph of solar fire.   5
Girth-high the poppies and the daisies
To brush the belly of my mule:
The thyme was smoking up God's praises,
The sun was warm, the wind was cool,
The white sierra was the icy   10
Refrigerator of that noon
And in that air so fresh, so spicy,
So steep, so pale, Toledo's June,
The sun seemed smaller than the moon.
Wading through seas of fire and blood   15
(I never saw such flowers before)
I said to Apis, 'What a cud
To make the bulls of Bashan roar!'
The church, with storks upon the steeple,
And scarcely could my cross be signed,   20
When round me came those Christian people
So hospitably clean, and kind.
Beans and Alfalfa in the manger—
Alfalfa, there was never such!
And rice and rabbit for the stranger.   25
Thank you very much!

[1935. *ME* (as 'Thank You Very Much'), *CP* II]

The Sling

GUARDING the cattle on my native hill
This was my talisman. Its charm was known
High in the blue and aquiline ozone,
And by my tireless armourer, the rill,
Smoothing his pellets to my hand or eye: 5
And how its meteors sang into the sky
The eagles of the Berg remember still.

I wore this herdsman's bracelet all day long:
To me it meant 'To-morrow' and 'Perhaps',
The insults of Goliath, his collapse,   10
Much fighting, and (who knows?) a life of song.
So fine a jewel at his wrist to swing
(For it was Chance) has seldom graced a king—
As I have dangled on a rawhide thong.

It spelt me luck in every polished stone   15
That to its mark, or thereabouts, had won:
For it had been to a poor herdsman's son
A stirrup once, to vault into a throne
And ride a nation over its despair;
To me, it seemed an amulet of prayer,   20
Remembering David and the warrior Joan.

I thought of the incendiary hope
Such herdsmen brought to cities from the hills,
Taught by the rash example of the rills,
Leaping in fire, to rush the headlong slope,   25
To gather impetus for height that's lost,
And hurtle through, regardless of the cost,
Where cunning or precaution have no scope.

When I have felt the whiff of madness' wing,
And rioted in barrios of shame,   30
Where all they gave me was a thirsty flame,
To burn my lips, that could no longer sing—
Around my fevered pulse to cool the flame,
There ghosted at my wrist an airy sling
And drew me to a garden, or a spring.   35

68

My link, in its long absence, with delight:
My handcuff (if I looked upon a knife)
That chained me to the miracle of life
Through a long frost and winter of the sprite:
And ready, at most need, to arm my prayer,   40
As once, when cries and feathers filled the air,
It saved a silver egret from a kite.

When stranded on these unfamiliar feet
Without a horse, and in the Stranger's land,
Like any tamest Redneck to your hand,   45
I shuffled with the Charlies in the street
Forgetting I was born a Centaur's foal;
When like the rest, I would have sawn my soul
Short at the waist, where man and mount should meet—

Its tightened thong would jerk me to control,   50
And never let the solar memory set
Of those blue highlands which are Eden yet
For all the rage of dynamite or coal—
Whose sunrise is the vision that I see then,
That, hurled like Bruce's heart amongst the heathen, 55
Leads on our White Commando to its goal!

Where none break ranks though down the whole race treks,
It taught me how to separate, and choose;
The uniform they ordered, to refuse—
The hornrimmed eyes, the ringworm round their necks; 60
And, when the Prince of herdsmen rode on high,
To rope those hikers with that bolshie tie,
To save my scruff, and see without the specs:—

Choosing my pebbles (to distinguish, free)
I had dispensed with numbers; finding how,   65
Since Space was always Here as Time was Now,
Extent of either means a Fig to me;
To the whole field I can prefer a flower
And know that States are foundered by an hour
While centuries may groan to fell a tree.   70

By its cool guidance I unread my books
And learned, in spite of theories and charts,
Things have a nearer meaning to their looks
Than to their dead analyses in parts;
And how (for all the outfit be antique)   75
Our light is in our heads; and we can seek
The clearest information in our hearts.

It taught me to inflict or suffer pain:
That my worst fortune was to serve me right,
And though it be the fashion to complain,   80
Self-pity is the ordure of the sprite,
But faith its ichor; and though in my course,
A rival knot the grass to spill my horse,
That trusting all to luck is half the fight.

It taught me that the world is not for Use;   85
But is, to each, the fruit of his desire,
From whose superb Grenade to swill the juice,
Some thaw its rosy frost into a fire—
Leaving the husks they most expect to find
To those insisting on the horny rind;   90
For it rewards as we to it aspire.

So ripe a fruit, so ruddy, and so real!—
To-night it bleeds, as when in days gone by
(Aldebaran a rowel at my heel)
I rounded up the cattle on the sky   95
Against the Berg's Toledo-steepled walls—
As now, upon the mesas of Castile
Beside the city that it most recalls.

For him whose teeth can crack the bitter rind—
Still to his past the future will reply,   100
And build a sacred city in his mind
With singing towers to thunder in the wind:
To light his life will shine the herdsman King
Who whirls our great Pomegranate in his sling
To herd the other planets through the sky.   105

Slung at his wrist will hang the phantom stress
Of David's stone—to weigh that all is right;
Even to daunt him should the weak unite
In one Goliath, he'll accept and bless,
Whose home's the Earth, and Everywhere his bed   110
A sheepskin saddle to his seat or head,
And Here and Now his permanent address.

[*ME, CP* I]

Rust

SEE there, and there it gnaws, the Rust—
Voet-ganger*of the coming swarm
Whose winged innumerable storm
Shall grind their pylons into dust.

Whose dropped asphyxiating dung   5
Shall fall exploding blood and mire;
Whose cropping teeth of rattled fire
Shall make one cud of old and young;—

Till turning from the carnage then
Themselves in anger to devour,   10
Shall die a race of weary men—

And all to spring the dainty flower
That, herding on that blasted heath,
A cowboy chews between his teeth.

[*ME, CP* I]

* *Voet-ganger:* newly-hatched locust—'Foot-goer'. [RC]

Junction of Rails: Voice of the Steel

CITIES of cinemas and lighted bars,
Smokers of tall bituminous cigars,
Whose evenings are a smile of golden teeth—
Upon your cenotaphs I lay this wreath
And so commend you to the moon and stars.   5

For I attain your presence in the dark
Deriding gossip Reuter's twittered spark
And reach you rails that, swifter in career,
Arrive as due as they depart from here—
I am a tour on which the hours embark.   10

Through me the moon, in ruled meridian steel,
Unwinding journeys from a burnished reel,
Stitches the world with threads of fire: each clue,
Pulleyed with rolling-stock as webs with dew,
A nerve for sleeping capitals to feel.   15

Their life-blood circulating in my veins,
With runnelled iron I irrigate the plains
And spider touring metal through the rock,
While to the same tentacular tick-tock
My scarecrow signals semaphore their trains.   20

Under this bleak mechanical display
I screen an inward knowledge, when the day
X-rays the fingers of my open hand
Over the chess-board acres of the land
Whose towns are shifted peons in the play.   25

Progress, the blue macadam of their dream,
Its railed and shining hippodrome of steam,
Glazed by cool horsepower, varnished clean with wheels,
Filming their destiny in endless reels,
Defers the formal ending that they scheme.   30

They greet each other in these gliding cars,
Read the same nightly journal of the stars,
And when the rail rings I can hear the bells
Ringing for dinner in the world's hotels
And after that the closing of the bars. 35

Though they have taught the lightning how to lie
And made their wisdom to misread the sky
I hold their pulses: through my ringing loom
Their trains with flying shuttles weave a doom
I am too sure a prophet to defy. 40

And when they jargon through the wind and rain
Breathing false hopes upon a frosty pane,
I hear the sad electrocuted words
Thud from the wires like stiffly-frozen birds
That warming hands resuscitate in vain. 45

The de Profundis of each canine hell
Voices their needs in its voluptuous swell:
While from the slums the radio's hollow strain
From hungry guts ventriloquizing pain
Belies them, as it sobs that all is well. 50

Then like a flawless magnet to the fact
Into my secret knowledge I attract
Their needles of dissimulated fear
Whose trembling fingers indicate me here
The focus of their every mood and act. 55

What hopes are theirs, what knowledge they forgo
From day to day procrastinating woe—
I, balancing each project and desire,
Funambulize upon my strands of fire
Too many aspirations not to know. 60

I am the plexus of their myriad schemes,
And were I flesh the ruin would undo me
Of all the purposes they sinew through me,
Of thwarted embassies, and beaten teams,
And home-returning honeymoons as gloomy. 65

How shrill the long hosannas of despair
With which those to-fro scolopendras bear,
Statesmen to conferences, troops to war—
All that concerted effort can restore
Like rattled cans to porters of despair!   70

But in the waiting-room where Time has beckoned
His vanguard, every moment must be reckoned
And fierce anticipation push the clock
Though for each same reiterated second
The whole world swing its pendulum of rock.   75

Far on the plain my waving pennons stream,
In the blue light the white horsetailing steam:
Or where they storm the night with rosy cirrus—
(Armoured incendiary, plumy Pyrrhus!)
Through palaces of ice where eagles scream.   80

From fog-red docks, the sink of rotting drains,
Where, tipsy giants, reel the workless cranes:
Where in dead liners, that the rust attacks,
Sprung decks think back beyond the saw and axe,
And masts put on the green of country lanes—   85

I tentacle the news: relay the mails:
And sense the restive anger that prevails
Wherever shafts descend or girders rise:
And day and night their steel-to-steel replies
Hum in my bolts and tingle in my rails.   90

These tons of metal rusting in the rain
(Iron on strike) are singing one refrain:
Let steel hang idle, burning rust devour,
Till Beauty smile upon the face of Power
And Love unsheathe me from the rust again . . .   95

My rails that rove me through the whispered corn
Bring me the tidings of a world unborn:
My sleepers escalading to the skies
Beyond the far horizons seems to rise
And form a Jacob's ladder to the morn.   100

And I often thought by lonely sidings—
What shepherd or what cowboy in his ridings
Forges the Sword so terrible and bright
That brings not peace, but fury of delight,
And of whose coming I have had the tidings.   105

They are the tidings of a world's relief:
My aching rails run out for their belief
To where a halted Star or rising Crescent
Above a byre or sheepfold hangs quiescent,
And meditation reaps the golden sheaf—   110

The joy that veld and kopje thrice restored
To that bleak wilderness the city horde—
When once the living radios of God,
By ravens fed, the lonely places trod,
And talked with foxes, and with lions roared.   115

A sword is singing and a scythe is reaping
In those great pylons prostrate in the dust,
Death has a sword of valour in his keeping
To arm our souls towards the future leaping:
And holy holy holy is the rust   120
Wherein the blue Excaliburs are sleeping!

[Begun August 1933, completed July 1936. *ME, CP* I]

In Memoriam of 'Mosquito', my partner in the horse-trade, gipsy of the Lozoya Clan

I never felt such glory
As handcuffs on my wrists.
My body stunned and gory
With toothmarks on my fists:
The triumph through the square,   5
My horse behind me led,
A pistol at my cutlets
Three rifles at my head:

75

And four of those Red bastards
To hold one wounded man   10
To all the staring rabble
Proclaiming thus my clan.
Then in the high grey prison
They threw me on the straw,
And through the grille beside me,   15
Beyond the bridge, I saw
Our other horse 'Gaona',
Across the sand-hills fled
With empty saddle: then I knew,
'Mosquito', you were dead,   20
And low on the meseta
The sun was turning red.
Across the desert sand-hills
It slowly bled from sight,
And, like a horse, a huge black wind   25
Fled screaming through the night.

> [1936. *ME* (as 'To my Jockey'), *CP* II (in
> this altered version)]

To Mary after the Red Terror

When the anopheles were blithe
And life with fever played the whore:
And Death was plying at his scythe
Like a great oarsman at his oar:

And all along that fearful trip   5
That scorned the vengeance of the past,
I saw the world, a sinking ship,
As from the summit of its mast:

Dingdonging in the lunar steeple
Of madness, with a wound to nurse,   10
For food and drink I asked the people
But all they gave me was a curse:

76

Then when we strays were roped and branded
(A burning cross upon the breast)
And in the old Corral were landed   15
Survivors of the rinderpest,—

You led me to the feet of Christ
Who threatened me with lifted quirt:
But by its loving fury sliced
I staggered upright from the dirt: 20

And that is why I do not simper,
Nor sigh, nor whine in my harangue.
Instead of ending with a whimper,
My life will finish with a bang!

[*ME* (as 'To Mary'), *CP* II (cut)]

Toledo, July 1936

TOLEDO, when I saw you die
And heard the roof of Carmel crash,
A spread-winged phoenix from its ash
The cross remained against the sky!
With horns of flame and haggard eye   5
The mountain vomited with blood,
A thousand corpses down the flood
Were rolled gesticulating by,
And high above the roaring shells
I heard the silence of your bells   10
Who've left these broken stones behind
Above the years to make your home,
And burn, with Athens and with Rome,
A sacred city of the mind.

[August 1936. *ME*, *CP* I]

Hot Rifles

OUR rifles were too hot to hold,
The night was made of tearing steel,
And down the street the volleys rolled
Where as in prayer the snipers kneel.
From every cranny, rift, or creek,   5
I heard the fatal furies scream,
And the moon held the river's gleam
Like a long rifle to its cheek.
Of all that fearful fusillade
I reckoned not the gain or loss   10
To see (her every forfeit paid)
And grander, though her riches fade,
Toledo, hammered on the Cross,
And in her Master's wounds arrayed.

[1936. *ME, CP* I]

Christ in Uniform

CLOSE at my side a girl and boy
Fell firing, in the doorway here,
Collapsing with a strangled cheer
As on the very couch of joy,
And onward through a wall of fire   5
A thousand others rolled the surge,
And where a dozen men expire
A hundred myrmidons emerge—
As if the Christ, our Solar Sire,
Magnificent in their intent,   10
Returned the bloody way he went,
Of so much blood, of such desire,
And so much valour proudly spent,
To weld a single heart of fire.

[*ME* (as 'Christs in Uniform'), *CP* I]

78

The Alcazar Mined

THIS Rock of Faith, the thunder-blasted—
Eternity will hear it rise
With those who (Hell itself out-lasted)
Will lift it with them to the skies!
Till whispered through the depths of Hell   5
The censored Miracle be known,
And flabbergasted Fiends re-tell
How fiercer tortures than their own
By living faith were overthrown;
How mortals, thinned to ghastly pallor,   10
Gangrened and rotting to the bone,
With winged souls of Christian valour
Beyond Olympus or Valhalla
Can heave ten thousand tons of stone!

[1936. *ME* (as 'The Alcazar'), *CP* I]

A Good Resolution

ENOUGH of those who study the oblique,
Inverted archaeologists, who seek
The New, as if it were some quaint antique—

Nomads of Time, and pungent with its must,
Who took the latest crinolines on trust   5
As wigwams for their vagrant wanderlust;—

Of jargons that a fuddled Celt will mix
By the blue light of methylated wicks,
Fishing dead words like kippers from the Styx;—

Sham Brownings, too, who'll cloud a shallow stream,   10
Or in a haystack hide a needle theme
Till platitudes like propositions seem—

With *pontes asinorum* bridging ditches
That, fully-armed, without the aid of witches,
Old knights could hurdle in their cast-iron breeches.   15

Hide poverty beneath a chequered shirt
And trust from common eyesight to divert
The jagged ribs that corrugate the dirt.

I will go stark: and let my meanings show
Clear as a milk-white feather in a crow   20
Or a black stallion on a field of snow.

[ME, CP I]

Selection from *Flowering Rifle*

How thrilling sweet, as in the dawn of Time,
Under our horses smokes the pounded thyme
As we go forward; streaming into battle   3585
Down on the road the crowded lorries rattle
Wherein the gay blue-shirted boys are singing,
As to a football match the rowdies bringing—
But of this match the wide earth is the ball
And by its end shall Europe stand or fall: 3590
Cresting the rise, through dimly vapoured screens,
We hear the crackle of the death-machines,
But dwarfed by height and distance, it might be
A summer veld-fire that we hear and see,
Which drought, or some Red labourer set alight   3595
To spoil the pasture or revenge a slight.
Through rolling smokewreaths, there, like ant-hills, rise
The koppies in the nitre-breathing skies,
While, in the troops, we see such turmoil reign
As in the tiny creatures of the plain.   3600
Now like singed beetles lurch the coming Tanks
Followed by seeming ants, amid whose ranks
Fall cinders as they simmer here and there
Blown sidelong by the whiffs of torrid air,

As heat had brought them humming from their hives 3605
To save their hoarded harvests with their lives—
But steel the harvest, bullets are the grain
They gather there in gaping jaws of pain.
While in the air with equal skill and ease,
Performing on their terrible trapeze, 3610
The cruising gun-birds trim the sunny breeze,
Like swifts, and rollers, and meropidae,
Whom burning grass has lured from far away,
When through the smoke each fork-tailed beauty flies
To hawk the roasted insects as they rise. 3615
Past dead men lying nonchalantly round
As if in brief siestas on the ground,
The horses, trotting, lift the town in view,
And thunder loudens, hammering the shoe
Of the Red Horse, so soon perhaps to pass, 3620
The world for pampa, with its men for grass,
Whose shrieking whinny now our spirits hear
As down the widened valley we career
To sweep the falling city in the rear.
Past wounded men returning back, whose cheer 3625
Rings like a ghostly whisper in the ear,
While to the left the rocky tempest raves
In which the cannon plough their jagged caves
And masonry is rumbled like the waves,
As if the world with undulating spine 3630
Would imitate the heavings of the brine,
While architecture flies in smithereens,
The houses cataract into ravines,
And the steep rampart, with a roll of thunder,
As a great dam had burst itself asunder, 3635
With men and rocks, a terrible moraine,
Goes avalanching downwards to the plain.
But nearer yet, and we are in the storm
Before their battered rearguard can reform—
While running bolshies fall upon their face, 3640
Some stop to fire, reloading as they race,
Suddenly doubling as you make their pace,
So where you thought to slash the bulging nape
It is a face you widen in its gape,

To whose fierce shock your jolted elbow rings   3645
And like a tuning-fork, your sabre sings,
The numbing blow, in its collected force,
Trebled by the momentum of the horse.

[Begun September 1937, completed March 1938.
Published 1939, and (substantially revised) in *CP* II]

The Clock in Spain

THIS Clock from England says he came
Where as a God he was revered.
His hours in length were all the same,
And each departed whence it came
The moment its relief appeared.   5

To a great Firm his line he traces,
Of manufacturers the aces,
And if you don't believe it's true,
The legend written on his face is
'Birmingham 1922'.   10

Squire was the Auden of those days
And Shanks the Spender of our trade:
For there the Clock awards the bays
And tells the prophets when to fade
Or die of one another's praise.   15

Like a policeman on his beat
The despot ticked with measured tread,
Dictating when to sleep, or eat,
Or drink—for in the darkest street
No Pub could open till he said.   20

Hours never telescoped in one
Disjointed by the lovers' thrill,
Nor made the night like water run
To strand the flushed and gasping sun,
Dumbfounded, on their window-sill.   25

Big Ben proclaimed, through mists of grime,
The surly fascism of Time,
And all the small Benitos, then,
Would cuckoo, tinkle, chirp, or chime
Their orders to the race of men.   30

Some Red Brigadier, panic-shod,
Abandoned here, on Spanish sod,
This sacred fetish of his race
He'd fought to substitute for God—
So we took pity on his case: 35

And placed him on the mantel here,
Where still he ticked with might and main,
Though, like his countrymen, in vain,
With local ways to interfere
And stop the history of Spain.   40

The Sun would pause to hear a song
And loiter, when he chose to chime,
Which always put him in the wrong:
And folk would dance the whole night long
When he proclaimed it closing time.   45

His heart was broken by the trains
Which left him panting hours ahead:
And he was liable to sprains,
For on the wall we knocked his brains
Each time he shrilled us out of bed.   50

Like Bonaparte upon his isle
Confronted by Sir Hudson Lowe,
The Despot lost his haughty style
Recalling with a rueful dial
His pomp and pride of long ago.   55

But when, athwart an open door,
He smelt the orange-trees in flower,
And heard the headlong Tagus roar,
And saw the white sierras soar,
That moment cost him half an hour.   60

And when amidst the poplars white
He heard the nightingales unite
To drown the torrent's hoarse furore,
And held his breath from sheer delight—
It lost him fifty minutes more!   65

About the time of our Fiesta,
When gales from the meseta sweep
To strew the roses fetlock-deep—
He fell into his first siesta,
And now he often has a sleep.   70

But what served most to change his story
And turn his notions outside in—
This clock so querulous and hoary
Beheld my love, in all her glory,
Clearing for action to the skin: 75

Her hair that smokes with raven swirl
To tell of banked and hidden fire,
And golden dynamos that whirl
To launch a battleship of pearl
Into the rollers of desire.   80

He saw her deep dark eyes ignite
Like radium, or the northern light
That through the blackening ether flies,
And to the voltage of delight
In glittering swordplay fall and rise.   85

Her eyelashes with jet-black sting
Like scorpions curved: and dark as night
The chevrons on her brows that spring
Like feathers in a condor's wing
Arching their splendour in the height: 90

The ivory, the jet, the coral,
The dainty groove that dints her back
To take the sting from every moral
And make each jealousy or quarrel
The fiercer aphrodisiac.   95

The lips that burn like crimson chillies:
The valleys where the thyme uncloses:
The haunches like a bounding filly's:
Her breasts like bruised and bouncing roses—
And all the rest a field of lilies!   100

The room revolving like a wheel,
The romp, the tussle, then the fight,
The croup of galloping delight
Where rapture rides with rowelled heel,
Without a bridle, through the night.   105

Since then our clock has ceased to rail
Or tick the time, as if he knew
Time cannot change or custom stale
Those roses roaring in the gale
That, as I rode, around me blew.   110

Today more tractable you'll find him
And less on edge than was his wont.
In sprays of lilac we've enshrined him:
He stops the moment that you wind him,
Then starts up ticking, if you don't.   115

And now the pastures breathe their spice,
Twinkling with thyme and fresh anemone,
That punctuality's a vice
He swears today—and what a price
To have to pay for world-hegemony!   120

So silent with his rusty bell,
This ancient veteran of the shelf,
Whom I can neither pawn nor sell,
Reminds me somewhat of myself,
And if you want the reason, well,   125

Although he may appear to you
To have renounced his race and era,
His steel is British, cold, and blue,
As ever flashed at Waterloo
Or held the line at Talavera.   130

And if the dreadful hour should chime
For British blood, and steel as grim,
My clock will wake, and tick the time,
And slope his arms and march—and I'm
The one to fall in step with him.   135

The loud fire-eating propheteers
Will cross the drink in craven fears,
Or worse, like vulture, crow, and kite-hawk,
Engage in money-making fight-talk
And pick the bones of fusiliers.   140

Coining the opulence of Babbitts,
Out of the cowardice of rabbits
And mealy kisses of Iscariot,
More plutocratic in their habits,
The more they woo the proletariat—   145

In vain you'll ask of them the hour
When zero has begun to chime,
And that which pushed this idle pen
Will strike it forth in bursts that rhyme,
The trigger-finger on the Bren.   150

[*TB, CP* II]

San Juan de la Cruz

To Eve Kirk

WHEN that brown bird, whose fusillading heart
Is triggered on a thorn the dark night through,
Has slain the only rival of his art
That burns, with flames for feathers, in the blue—
I think of him in whom those rivals met   5
To burn and sing, both bird and star, in one:
The planet slain, the nightingale would set
To leave a pyre of roses for the Sun.

86

His voice an iris through its rain of jewels—
Or are they tears, those embers of desire,   10
Whose molten brands each gust of song re-fuels?—
He crucifies his heart upon his lyre,
Phoenix of Song, whose deaths are his renewals,
With pollen for his cinders, bleeding fire!

[May 1942. TB, CP I]

One Transport Lost

WHERE, packed as tight as space can fit them
The soldiers retch, and snore, and stink,
It was no bunch of flowers that hit them
And woke them up, that night, to drink.

Dashing the bulkheads red with slaughter,   5
In the steep wash that swept the hold,
Men, corpses, kitbags, blood, and water,
Colliding and commingling rolled.

Some clung, like flies, in fear and wonder,
Clutched to the crossbeams, out of reach,   10
Till sprayed from thence by jets of thunder
That spouted rumbling from the breach.

In this new world of blast and suction,
The bulkhead tilted to a roof;
Friend aided friend—but to destruction,   15
And valour seemed its own reproof.

Forced by the pent explosive airs
In the huge death-gasp of its shell,
Or sucked, like Jonah, by their prayers
From forth that spiracle of Hell—   20

The ones that catapulated from it
Saw the whole hull reverse its dome,
Then ram the depths, like some huge comet,
Flood-lit with phosphorus and foam.

The shark and grampus might reprieve,   25
After their jaunt upon a raft,
The few that got Survivors' Leave—
But those who perished would have laughed!

Their fiercest thirst they've quenched and cupped,
And smashed the glass (this life of slaves!);   30
No hectoring Redcaps interrupt
Their fornication with the waves.

For us, this world of Joad and Julian,
The dithering of abortive schemes;
For them, the infinite, cerulean   35
Suspension of desires and dreams.

So save your Bait, you Bards and Thinkers!
For us who daren't refuse to chew
Hook, line, and swivel, trace and sinkers,
And rod and all, and like it too!   40

For them, the wave, the melancholy
Chant of the wind that tells no lies;
The breakers roll their funeral volley
To which the thundering cliff replies.

The black cape-hens in decent crêpe   45
Will mourn them till the Last Event;
The roaring headlands of the Cape
Are lions on their monument.

[*TB, CP* II]

88

Nyanza Moonrise

AURORA to herself, whose white
Meridian, later, was my noon,
And then the dewed approach of night,
And then the rising of the moon.
That these four women were the same,   5
Though each was of the former born,
This moon reminds me now, whose flame
Bridges an absence as forlorn
Till, like her prayers, the far-shot rays,
Burnish my rifle, touch my brow,   10
And rule a pathway for my prow
Between the reefs and rocky bays,
With all Nyanza one round eye
To gaze her glory up the sky.

[May 1943. *TB, CP* II]

Snapshot of Nairobi

WITH orange-peel the streets are strown
And pips, beyond computing
On every shoulder save my own,
That's fractured with saluting.

[May 1943. *TB, CP* I]

Luis de Camões

CAMÕES, alone, of all the lyric race,
Born in the black aurora of disaster,
Can look a common soldier in the face:
I find a comrade where I sought a master:
For daily, while the stinking crocodiles   5
Glide from the mangroves on the swampy shore,
He shares my awning on the dhow, he smiles,
And tells me that he lived it all before.

Through fire and shipwreck, pestilence and loss,
Led by the ignis fatuus of duty   10
To a dog's death—yet of his sorrows king—
He shouldered high his voluntary Cross,
Wrestled his hardships into forms of beauty,
And taught his gorgon destinies to sing.

[June 1943. TB, CP I]

Imitation (and Endorsement) of the Famous Sonnet of Bocage which he Wrote on Active Service Out East

CAMÕES, great Camões! though twins in form
Tally the cursed fates that love to plague us,
Exchanging for our vineyards by the Tagus
The Sacrilegious Headland and the Storm:
Though, like yourself, from Chindwin to Zambezi   5
In wars and fearful penury I wander,
On vain desires my fevered sighs to squander,
And on the thorns of memory sleep uneasy:
Though trampled by the same vindictive doom,
I pray for sudden death to come tomorrow   10
And know that peace lies only in the tomb:
And though in shame and all precarious shifts
You were my model—mine's the crowning sorrow
To share your luck, but lack your towering gifts.

[June 1943. TB, CP II]

Dreaming Spires

THROUGH villages of yelping tykes
With skulls on totem-poles, and wogs
Exclaiming at our motor bikes
With more amazement than their dogs:

Respiring fumes of pure phlogiston   5
On hardware broncos, half-machine,
With arteries pulsing to the piston
And hearts inducting gasoline:

Buckjumping over ruts and boulders,
The Centaurs of an age of steel   10
Engrafted all save head and shoulders
Into the horsepower of the wheel—

We roared into the open country,
Scattering vultures, kites, and crows;
All Nature scolding our effrontery   15
In raucous agitation rose.

Zoology went raving stark
To meet us on the open track—
The whole riff raff of Noah's Ark
With which the wilderness was black.   20

With kicks and whinnies, bucks and snorts,
Their circuses stampeded by:
A herd of wildebeest cavorts,
And somersaults against the sky:

Across the stripes of zebras sailing,   25
The eyesight rattles like a cane
That's rattled down an area-railing
Until it blurs upon the brain.

The lions flee with standing hackles,
Leaving their feast before they've dined: 30
Their funeral poultry flaps and cackles
To share the breeze they feel behind.

Both wart- and road-hog vie together,
As they and we, petarding smoke,
Belly to earth and hell for leather,   35
In fumes of dust and petrol choke.

We catch the madness they have caught,
Stand on the footrests, and guffaw—
Till shadowed by a looming thought
And visited with sudden awe,   40

We close our throttles, clench the curb,
And hush the rumble of our tyres,
Abashed and fearful to disturb
The City of the Dreaming Spires—

The City of Giraffes!—a People   45
Who live between the earth and skies,
Each in his lone religious steeple,
Keeping a light-house with his eyes:

Each his own stairway, tower, and stylite,
Ascending on his saintly way   50
Up rungs of gold into the twilight
And leafy ladders to the day:

Chimneys of silence! at whose summit,
Like storks, the daydreams love to nest;
The Earth, descending like a plummet   55
Into the oceans of unrest,

They can ignore—whose nearer neighbour
The sun is, with the stairs and moon
That on their hides, with learned labour,
Tattooed the hieroglyphic rune.   60

Muezzins that from airy pylons
Peer out above the golden trees
Where the mimosas fleece the silence
Or slumber on the drone of bees:

Nought of this earth they see but flowers   65
Quilting a carpet to the sky
To where some pensive crony towers
Or Kilimanjaro takes the eye.

Their baser passions fast on greens
Where, never to intrude or push,   70
Their bodies live like submarines,
Far down beneath them, in the bush.

Around their head the solar glories,
With their terrestrial sisters fly—
Rollers, and orioles, and lories,   75
And trogons of the evening sky.

Their bloodstream with a yeasty leaven
Exalts them to the stars above,
As we are raised, though not to heaven,
By drink—or when we fall in love.   80

By many a dismal crash and wreck
Our dreams are weaned of aviation,
But these have beaten (by a neck!)
The steepest laws of gravitation.

Some animals have all the luck,   85
Who hurl their breed in nature's throat—
Out of a gumtree by a buck,
Or escalator—by a goat!

When I have worked my ticket, pension,
And whatsoever I can bum,   90
To colonize the fourth dimension,
With my Beloved, I may come,

And buy a pair of stilts for both,
And hire a periscope for two,
To vegetate in towering sloth   95
Out here amongst these chosen few . . .

Or so my fancies seemed to sing
To see, across the gulf of years,
The soldiers of a reigning King
Confront those ghostly halberdiers.   100

But someone kicks his starter back:
Anachronism cocks its ears.
Like Beefeaters who've got the sack
With their own heads upon their spears;

Like Leftwing Poets at the hint   105
Of work, or danger, or the blitz,
Or when they catch the deadly glint
Of satire, swordplay of the wits,—

Into the dusk of leafy oceans
They fade away with phantom tread;   110
And changing gears, reversing notions,
The road to Moshi roars ahead.

[March 1944. *TB, CP* I]

Heartbreak Camp

To Major S. C. Mason of the Nigerian Regiment

RED as the guardroom lamp
The moon inspects the trees:
High over Heartbreak Camp,
Orion stands at ease:

With buttons lit, for Sentry,   5
He challenges who's there
Acceding all the entry
Whose passport is Despair.

All joys are privates there
Who seldom go on leave   10
And only sorrows wear
Three chevrons on their sleeve:

But boredom wears three pips,
A fiend of monstrous size,
With curses on his lips   15
And circles round his eyes.

All round, for league on league
And labouring up the hills,
The clouds are on fatigue,
Collecting damps and chills.   20

Sir Dysentery Malaria,
A famous brigadier,
Commands the whole sub-area,
And stalking in his rear,

A more ferocious colonel   25
Lord Tremens (of the Drunks)
To whose commands infernal
We tremble in our bunks.

Here, till the pale aurora
Dismiss the stars from drill,   30
I dream of my Señora
Behind the guardroom grille.

In the outcry of crickets
And the silence of guitars,
I watch the lonely pickets   35
And the slow patrol of stars.

Our vineyard and the terrace
By the Tagus, they recall,
With the Rose of the Sierras,
Whom I love the best of all!   40

My heart was once her campfire
And burned for her alone,
Fed with the thyme and samphire
That azure days had grown.

My thoughts for their safari   45
Have scarcely taken wings
Through spaces wide and starry
To hear her stroke the strings:

But ere one word be spoken
A fiend my elbow jogs,   50
The reverie is broken
By the tomtom of the wogs:

And, all illusions killing,
Upon the stillness jars
A far hyaena drilling   55
His company of stars.

[*TB, CP* II]

Reflections

WHILE Echo pined into a shade,
Narcissus, by the water's shelf,
Met with a lurking death, and made
An alligator of himself.

Of many selves we all possess   5
My meanest has the most persisted,
The one that joined the N.F.S.
When half humanity enlisted.

A shifty and insidious ghost,
Of all my selves he is the one,   10
Though it's with him I meet the most,
I'd go the longest way to shun.

When manhood crests the full red stream
Of comradeship, and breasts the surge,
Dreaming a chilled, amphibious dream,   15
He haunts the shallows by the verge.

Out of the mirrors in hotels
He makes for me, but as I pass,
Recedes into their glazing wells
And leaves no ripples on the glass.   20

Along the windows of the shops,
And in the tankard's curving base,
I have surprised him as he drops
Into the void without a trace.

He shaves the surfaces: he snails   25
His sheeny track along the walls:
The windows seem a myriad scales
Through which an endless serpent crawls.

His form is one, his number legion:
He incubates in hushed platoons,   30
Denizens of the glassy region
And of the vitreous lagoons.

Each time I step into the street
I multiply his gliding swarms,
Along the panes to launch a fleet   35
Of bloodless and reptilian forms.

I know the scar upon his cheek,
His limp, his stare, his friendly smile—
Though human in his main physique,
Yet saurian in his lurking guile.   40

Well on this side of make-believe,
Though edging always to the flanks,
He wears my chevrons on his sleeve
As though he'd earned them in the ranks.

In him, behind each sheet of glaze,   45
A Eunuch with a bowstring hides:
Under each film, with lidless gaze,
A sleepless alligator slides.

Within his heart, so chilled and squamous,
He knows I've but to sell my pride   50
To make him safe, and rich, and famous;
And he would fatten if I died.

In feigned petition from the sash
He swerves to me, and I from him:
But if one day you hear a splash,   55
You'll know he's fastened on a limb.

No ripple on the glassy frame
Will show you where a man was drowned;
But Echo, practising his Fame,
Will pine once more into a sound.   60

[July 1944. *TB, CP* I]

Washing Day

AMONGST the rooftop chimneys where the breezes
Their dizzy choreography design,
Pyjamas, combinations, and chemises
Inflate themselves and dance upon the line.
Drilled by a loose disorder and abandon,   5
They belly and explode, revolve and swing,
As fearless of the precipice they stand on
As if there were religion in a string.
Annexing with their parachute invasion
The intimate behaviour of our life,   10
They argue, or embrace with kind persuasion,
And parody our dalliance or our strife.
We change ideas and moods like shirts or singlets,
Which, having shed, they rise to mock us still:
And the wind laughs and shakes her golden ringlets   15
To set them independent of our will.

They curtsey and collapse, revolve and billow—
A warning that, when least aware we lie,
The dreams are incubated in our pillow
That animate its chrysalis to fly.   20

[*TB, CP* I]

On the Martyrdom of F. Garcia Lorca

NOT only did he lose his life
By shots assassinated:
But with a hatchet and a knife
Was after that—translated.

[*TB, CP* I]

Rhapsody of the Man in Hospital Blues and the 'Hyde Park Lancers'

To the Memory of R.S.M. Charles Mulvey of
Princess Pat's Canadian Light Infantry

FROM Notting Hill to Prince's Gate
I'd started breaking-in my stick
And of my new, three-legged gait
Acquired the quaint arithmetic.

No more to canter, trot or trippel,   5
Where dandies prance along the Row,
I coaxed the strange unwieldy cripple
I had become yet feared to know:

In spite of one so ill-adjusted,
So keenly to the task he warmed,   10
So eagerly to me he trusted,
So newly had he been deformed,

99

That though he seemed a drunken lout,
Less of a comrade than a weight,
I had no further choice or doubt   15
But to accept him as my fate.

(So old Sinbad to ruth was wrought
When, thus accosted for a lift,
A chronic pickaback he caught
From the old scrounger by the Drift.)   20

Then as I pondered this new trouble
Which he'd confided to my care,
Six others passed us, bending double,
Who seemed our fellowship to share—

For in their style was nothing alien,   25
Those Hyde-Park Lancers, dressed to stun,
In great cocked hats, with slouch Australian,
Though plume or chinstrap they had none.*

Like grim knights-errant on their journey,
Couching their broomsticks tipped with pins,   30
I watched them joust their dismal tourney
Tentpegging garbage into tins.

Identically armed and hatted,
We prodded grimly as we bent:
No last-man-in has ever batted   35
With a more desperate intent.

In the same action were our talents
Employed, though in a different stead,
Since I was prodding for my balance
And they were prodding for their bread.   40

* The name given by soldiers to the Sanitary Scavengers of London County
Council. They used to wear hats slightly resembling those worn by the author's
regiment, the King's African Rifles, but without the bunch of feathers and the
chinstrap. [RC]

Gone was the thunder of great herds,
Lost was the lilt of marching men,
And void the bandolier of words
That feeds the rifle of my pen.

I listened with my six companions   45
To the low hum of our environ,
And London's streets, like roaring canyons,
With streams of whisky, blood and iron.

Amongst the leafless trees that froze
The wind struck up with flute and fife   50
The regimental march of those
Who've fallen out of step with life.

We must be silent when men mutter,
We must keep calm when tempers rise,
And when we're shoved into the gutter   55
It's we who must apologise.

To have one's Cross laid on inside
Abates no ardour in the strife
Though something in us might have died
Yet something more had come to life.   60

[Begun 1945, completed June 1950. *CP* II]

Ballad of Don Juan Tenorio and the Statue
of the Comendador

TEN cuckolds, slain without confession
In duels, by the waterfront
Of Hades, in a glum procession
Are singing out for Charon's punt.

Ten weeping women dry their clothes   5
Washed up along the homeless sands
By the red sea of perjured oaths
That shoals with amputated hands.

These were the fruits of all your swagger!
But through their tears will swim no more   10
Those ice-cold fish, your sword and dagger,
Whose fin-wake is a streak of gore;

For now the hour is aiming at you,
Tenorio! with its finger hooked:
Remember when you cuffed the statue   15
Upon the grave: and how it looked:

And how it seemed to nod its head
When you invited it to dine.
If you were wise to tempt the dead
You verify to-night, at nine.   20

The stars are like cicadas chirping
With cold: but it is snug in here,
The throne of opulence usurping,
Beneath this costly chandelier.

The firelight twinkles on the jewels   25
Of pistol-butts: the rays enthrall
The glinting cutlery of duels
That hang for trophies round the wall.

Your Rolls sleeps safely in its garage,
Your Derby-winner in his stall: 30
But with a prayer balloon your barrage
Against the doom that's due to fall.

Pay off your cook and sack your butler:
Renounce your sacrilegious vow:
Though Satan were Toledo's cutler   35
No swordplay could avail you now.

A sentence Lawyers cannot garble
Has just been read: the tombs are still:
But from their garrisons of marble
One headstone moves along the hill.   40

The wind begins to grow much colder,
The grass with icicles to clink:
To pedestal the skating boulder
Each rivulet becomes a rink.

The river bridged itself with crystal   45
To its refrigerating tread.
The moon rose masked, and cocked the pistol
Of silence to the world's bald head.

Its passing starched the breath of bulls
Along the Guadalquivir's shore,   50
And froze the ferryman who pulls
More at his wineskin than his oar.

It seems your hounds have scented trouble.
The room grows arctic: moments drag:
Tenorio! pour yourself a double   55
To entertain the stalking crag.

Tenorio! it's too late for banter,
The statue knocks; the door gives way:
The whisky froze in the decanter
And has not melted to this day.   60

One handshake: then the detonation:
A stench of nitre fills the hall:
The Butler on investigation
Retrieved one tiepin: that was all.

Out to the tombs the Civil Guard   65
Followed the clues of all they heard.
But though one hand seemed slightly charred,
The statue would not speak one word.

[CP II]

103

Fishing Boats in Martigues

AROUND the quays, kicked off in twos
The Four Winds dry their wooden shoes.

[July 1953. *CP* II]

Jousé's Horses

To Frédéric Mistral, Neveu

COASTING the delta of the dead lagoons,
The patron said 'We're in for dirty weather.
See, here come Jousé's horses, all together,
(Confound the vermin!) making for the dunes.'

And there along the low verge of the land   5
All silver fire, (Niagara set free!)
A hundred silken streamers swept the sand,
And with them came the wind, and rose the sea!

[*CP* II]

Félibre

To Frédéric Mistral, Neveu

OF all the immortality-concoctors
Who cook their would-be by their midnight lamps—
They blame me that I shun my fellow-doctors
To haunt the quays, the markets, and the camps.

Yeats on his intellect could pull the blinds   5
Rapping up spooks. He fell for freaks and phoneys.
Weird blue-stockings with damp, flatfooted minds,
Theosophists and fakirs, were his cronies.

I, too, can loose my Pegasus to graze,
Carouse with drunken fiddlers at the Fair,   10
And with the yokelry on market days
Jingle in spurs and sheepskins round the square.

They say it is a waste of time. I differ.
To learn should be as easy as to look.
You could not pass examinations stiffer,   15
Nor sweat a deeper learning from the book—

Than to be passed for native by the million
When chiming in at horsefairs with my bid.
This taught me the Gallego and Castilian
By which I know my 'Lusiads' and the 'Cid'.   20

Comradeship, though it's dated and antique,
Is all the Anthropology I know.
The Zulu and Swahili that I speak
I learned no more than water learned to flow.

Collective writers at my name grow raucous,   25
And pedants raise a loud indignant cry
Like the New Critics and the Kenyon caucus—
Or poultry, when a falcon cruises by!

I've had my share of solitudes and caverns.
What mountain-tops could teach I learned of old,   30
But got the true Provençal in the taverns
By which I sailed into the 'Isles of Gold'.*

To sit with Mistral under the green laurels
From which his children gathered me my crown,†
While the deep wine that is the end of quarrels   35
Glows through me like the sunset going down.

                                        [1955. CP II]

* The title of Mistral's Lyrical Poems, 'Lis Isclo d'Or.' [RC]
  † The Crown of a 'Soci dou Felibrige': awarded to the author at Avignon 1953 by
the poets of the Provençal Language. [RC]

In Memoriam A. F. Tschiffely*

(Whose remains were carried to his grave on horseback in Buenos
Aires.)

ONLY a week before you died, we stood,
Gene Tunney and myself, on Stamford station
And voted it was worth a celebration
To drink the health of one so great and good:
We did not know how near to death you lay,   5
And as the train rolled onward through New York,
Each from his memories drew forth the cork
To which you are the vintage and bouquet.
Now from familiar talk to public greatness
Death hustles you. The long processions start.   10
You populate a Nation's mind and heart
In which your loss is felt as your innateness.
Through silent crowds the muffled drums ring hollow;
Behind your panthered horse, ten thousand strong,
True horsemen of Apollo, skilled in song,   15
The Gauchos, in their full regalia, follow.
Spread condors fly half-mast along the spine
Of both Americas. More dark and lonely
The pampa dreams tonight. Not Violet only
Is left a widow, but the Argentine.   20
You, like the Cid, are carried in the saddle
After your death. But spreading love, not fear,
Through all the plains and peaks that held you dear,
Today it is a Continent you straddle,
Whose soul in this strange Pegasus is hid   25
Tigered with dazzling scripts, in black and white,
Of all the poems that you did not write
But lived as deathlessly as if you did:
A continent whose elements aspire
To form this prancing symbol of its mind—   30
A Cross-breed less of Earth than Wave and Wind
And less of either than of dancing Fire:

---

* Aimé Felix Tschiffely (author of *Tschiffely's Ride*) was one of RC's close friends
after World War II. He died in London in 1954.

A torrent of white flame and jetblack stars,
A gust of the Pampero's snorted fumes,
A breaker from that sea of waving plumes   35
Whose skyline is a spangle of guitars,
Whose shoreline is the sunset in the west
Whence cloudy horsemen, Angels of the Andes,
Ride out to welcome you—peerless Hernandez,
Chocano, Don Roberto,† and the rest!   40

[Late 1954. Not previously collected]
† Hernandez (Argentine pronunciation) and Chocano: South American poets.
Don Roberto: Robert Cunninghame Graham. [RC]

November Nights

ON the westmost point of Europe, where it blows with might and
   main,
While loudly on the village-spires the weathercocks are shrieking,
And gusty showers, like kettledrums, are rattled on the pane,
The rafters like the shrouds of some old sailing-ship are creaking,
And the building reels and rumbles as it rides the wind and rain. 5

The treetops clash their antlers in their ultimate dishevelry:
The combers crash along the cliffs to swell the dreadful revelry,
And to the nightlong blaring of the lighthouse on the rocks
The fog-horns of the ships reply. The wolves in all their devilry,
Starved out of the sierras, have been slaughtering the flocks.   10

Now peasants shun the muddy fields, and fisherfolk the shores.
It is the time the weather finds the wounds of bygone wars,
And never to a charger did I take as I have done
To cantering the rocking-chair, my Pegasus, indoors,
For my olives have been gathered and my grapes are in the tun. 15

Between the gusts the wolves raise up a long-drawn howl of woe:
The mastiff whines, with bristled hair, beside us cowering low,
But for the firelight on your face I would not change the sun,
Nor would I change a moment of our winter-season, no,   20
For our springtime with its orioles and roses long ago.

[CP II]

TRANSLATIONS

Upon a Gloomy Night

[after Saint John of the Cross]

UPON a gloomy night,
With all my cares to loving ardours flushed,
(O venture of delight!)
With nobody in sight
I went abroad when all my house was hushed.   5

In safety, in disguise,
In darkness up the secret stair I crept,
(O happy enterprise)
Concealed from other eyes
When all my house at length in silence slept.   10

Upon that lucky night
In secrecy, inscrutable to sight,
I went without discerning
And with no other light
Except for that which in my heart was burning.   15

It lit and led me through
More certain than the light of noonday clear
To where One waited near
Whose presence well I knew,
There where no other presence might appear.   20

Oh night that was my guide!
Oh darkness dearer than the morning's pride,
Oh night that joined the lover
To the beloved bride
Transfiguring them each into the other.   25

Within my flowering breast
Which only for himself entire I save
He sank into his rest
And all my gifts I gave
Lulled by the airs with which the cedars wave.   30

Over the ramparts fanned
While the fresh wind was fluttering his tresses,
With his serenest hand
My neck he wounded, and
Suspended every sense with its caresses.   35

Lost to myself I stayed
My face upon my lover having laid
From all endeavour ceasing:
And all my cares releasing
Threw them amongst the lilies there to fade.   40

[June 1942. *TB, CP* I (as 'En Una Noche Oscura'),
St John, CP III]

Verses written after an ecstasy of high exaltation

[after Saint John of the Cross]

I ENTERED in. I know not where,
And I remained, though knowing naught,
Transcending knowledge with my thought.

Of when I entered I know naught,
But when I saw that I was there   5
(Though where it was I did not care)
Strange things I learned, with greatness fraught.
Yet what I heard I'll not declare.
But there I stayed, though knowing naught,
Transcending knowledge with my thought.   10

Of peace and piety interwound
This perfect science had been wrought,
Within the solitude profound
A straight and narrow path it taught,
Such secret wisdom there I found   15
That there I stammered, saying naught,
But topped all knowledge with my thought.

So borne aloft, so drunken-reeling,
So rapt was I, so swept away,
Within the scope of sense or feeling   20
My sense or feeling could not stay.
And in my soul I felt, revealing,
A sense that, though its sense was naught,
Transcended knowledge with my thought.

The man who truly there has come   25
Of his own self must shed the guise;
Of all he knew before the sum
Seems far beneath that wondrous prize:
And in this lore he grows so wise
That he remains, though knowing naught,   30
Transcending knowledge with his thought.

The farther that I climbed the height
The less I seemed to understand
The cloud so tenebrous and grand
That there illuminates the night.   35
For he who understands that sight
Remains for aye, though knowing naught,
Transcending knowledge with his thought.

This wisdom without understanding
Is of so absolute a force   40
No wise man of whatever standing
Can ever stand against its course,
Unless they tap its wondrous source,
To know so much, though knowing naught,
They pass all knowledge with their thought.   45

This summit all so steeply towers
And is of excellence so high
No human faculties or powers
Can ever to the top come nigh.
Whoever with its steep could vie,   50
Though knowing nothing, would transcend
All thought, forever, without end.

If you would ask, what is its essence—
This summit of all sense and knowing:
It comes from the Divinest Presence—   55
The sudden sense of Him outflowing,
In His great clemency bestowing
The gift that leaves men knowing naught,
Yet passing knowledge with their thought.

[*St John, CP* III]

With a divine intention

[after Saint John of the Cross]

WITHOUT support, yet well supported,
Though in pitch-darkness, with no ray,
Entirely I am burned away.
My spirit is so freed from every
Created thing, that through the skies,   5
Above herself, she's lifted, flies,
And as in a most fragrant reverie,
Only on God her weight applies.
The thing which most my faith esteems
For this one fact will be reported—   10
Because my soul above me streams
Without support, yet well supported.

What though I languish in the shades
As through my mortal life I go,
Not over-heavy is my woe,   15
Since if no glow my gloom invades,
With a celestial life I glow.
The love of such a life, I say,
The more benightedly it darkens,
Turns more to that to which it hearkens,   20
Though in pitch-darkness, with no ray.

Since I knew Love, I have been taught
He can perform most wondrous labours.
Though good and bad in me are neighbours
He turns their difference to naught   25
Then both into Himself, so sweetly,
And with a flame so fine and fragrant
Which now I feel in me completely
Reduce my being, till no vagrant
Vestige of my own self can stay.   30
And wholly I am burned away.

[St John, CP III]

Reyerta

[after Federico Garcia Lorca]

IN the midst of the ravine,
Glinting Albacete blades,
Beautified with rival bloods
Flash like fishes in the shades.
A hard flat light of playing cards   5
Outlines, against the bitter green,
Shapes of infuriated horses
And profiles of equestrian mien.

Under the branches of an olive,
Weep two women bent with age,   10
While the bull of altercation
Clambers up the walls with rage.
Black angels come with handkerchiefs
And water from the snowline-boulders,
Angels with vast wings, like the blades   15
Of Albacete, on their shoulders.
Juan Antonio from Montilla
Down the slope goes rolling dead,
With his flesh stuck full of lilies,
A sliced pomegranate for his head;   20
And now the cross of fire ascends
Along the highways of the dead.

The Judge and Civil Guard their way
Along the olive orchard take,
Where slithered blood begins to moan   25
The dumb song of an injured snake.
'Gentleman of the Civil Guard!
The same old story as before—
Five of the Carthaginians slain
And of the Roman people four.'   30
The maddening afternoon of figtrees
And of hot rumours, ending soon,
Fell down between the wounded thighs
Of the wild horsemen in a swoon.
Black angels fly across the air   35
From which the setting sun departs,
Angels with long dark streaming hair
And oil of olives in their hearts.

                              [*Lorca, CP* III]

114

Song of the Horseman

[after Federico Garcia Lorca]

CÓRDOBA.
Remote and lonely.

Jet-black mare and full round moon,
With olives in my saddle bags,
Although I know the road so well   5
I shall not get to Córdoba.

Across the plain, across the wind,
Jet-black mare and full red moon,
Death is gazing down upon me,
Down from the towers of Córdoba.   10

Ay! The road so dark and long.
Ay! My mare so tired yet brave.
Death is waiting for me there
Before I get to Córdoba.   15

Córdoba.
Remote and lonely.

                              [*Lorca*, CP III]

On the Skeleton of a Young Girl – after Rafael Morales

BETWEEN these brows, Oh God, between these brows
Clamoured the living flesh! Here in this bleak
Hollow is where the red blood used to rouse
The fleeting roses of a youthful cheek.

Just here, the cunning breast gave forth its bud,   5
Adventurously shy, with grace and charm.
Here a delightful hand once pulsed with blood—
The offspring of that non-existent arm!
Here also did the swanlike neck sustain
The plumèd solitude that was her brain,   10
Fledged with her curls, like pinions wide and fleet.
And here in plump and lazy warmth extended
Her legs, like forking rivers, till they ended
To find the wing'd resilience of her feet.

[CP III]

To a Millstone on the Ground—
Dionisio Ridruejo

THE straight race of the prisoned water turned
A circle, and became your voice and theme,
Round loaf of rock, whose floury dances churned
The waters, gay with duckweed, of the stream.

Sun of the grain-ears, whose rotating lips,   5
Lips of the plain, that lightly kissed the corn,
Now hush the bitter springtime to eclipse
Like a dead moon amongst the flowers that mourn.

Today you lie, a wayside seat, quite still
Old coin of memory, lost change that tumbles   10
Amidst the homeless wreckage of the mill . . .

Sad Cyclops, eye without a glance, blind stare:
Formed like our destiny that rolls and rumbles
Transfixed upon the axle of the air.

[CP III]

Toril

[after Rubén Darío]

CROWD   Another Bull! another Bull!

OX   You heard?
Your number's up, the people gave the word!

BULL   Feasted on flowers, the darling of the days,
To-day I've ghastly asphodels to graze,
Harsh sand to bite, and my own blood to swill—   5
Whose dewlap loved the golden-rolling rill,
When through the rushes, burnished like its tide,
The lovely cirrus of my thews would slide,
My heart flame-glazing through the silken skin
Joy of its mighty furnace lit within.   10
These crescent horns that scimitared the moon,
These eyes, the flaming emeralds of noon,
Whose orbs were fuel to the deathless rays
And burned the long horizon with their gaze—
All now to be cut down, and soon to trail   15
A sledge of carrion at a horse's tail!

OX   Flame in the flaming noon, I've seen you run.
The Anvil of Toledo's now your Sun,
Whose angry dawn beyond these gates has spread
Its crimson cape, the sunrise of the dead: 20
Whose iron clangs for you, whose doom you feel,
The target of its burnished ray of steel!

BULL   Ox as you are, what should you know of this
Who never neared the verge of that abyss?

OX   Ox as I am, none better knows than I   25
Who led your father's father here to die.
Declaiming clown, I am the mute, the wise;
Poets would read enigmas in my eyes.

My being is confederate with pain,
Mine to endure as yours is to complain;   30
I am the thinker, satisfied to know,
And bought this wisdom for a life of woe.
Be brave, be patient, and reserve your breath.

BULL   But tell me what is blacker than this Death?

OX   My impotence.

BULL   It was your soul that spoke!—   35
More hideous than this martyrdom?

OX   The Yoke!

[December 1933. *ME, CP I, CP III*]

The Albatross

[after Baudelaire]

SOMETIMES for sport the men of loafing crews
Snare the great albatrosses of the deep,
The indolent companions of their cruise
As through the bitter vastitudes they sweep.

Scarce have they fished aboard these airy kings   5
When helpless on such unaccustomed floors,
They piteously droop their huge white wings
And trail them at their sides like drifting oars.

How comical, how ugly, and how meek
Appears this soarer of celestial snows!   10
One, with his pipe, teases the golden beak,
One, limping, mocks the cripple as he goes.

118

The Poet, like this monarch of the clouds,
Despising archers, rides the storm elate.
But, stranded on the earth to jeering crowds,   15
The great wings of the giant baulk his gait.

[P, FR, CP I, Baudelaire, CP III]

The Giantess

[after Baudelaire]

OF old when Nature, in her verve defiant,
Conceived each day some birth of monstrous mien,
I would have lived near some young female giant
Like a voluptuous cat beside a queen;

To see her body flowering with her soul   5
Freely develop in her mighty games,
And in the mists that through her gaze would roll
Guess that her heart was hatching sombre flames;

To roam her mighty contours as I please,
Ramp on the cliff of her tremendous knees,   10
And in the solstice, when the suns that kill

Make her stretch out across the land and rest,
To sleep beneath the shadow of her breast
Like a hushed village underneath a hill.

[Baudelaire, CP III]

The Owls

[after Baudelaire]

WITHIN the shelter of black yews
The owls in ranks are ranged apart
Like foreign gods, whose eyeballs dart
Red fire. They meditate and muse.

Without a stir they will remain
Till, in its melancholy hour,
Thrusting the level sun from power,
The shade establishes its reign.

Their attitude instructs the sage,
Content with what is near at hand,
To shun all motion, strife, and rage.

Men, crazed with shadows that they chase,
Bear, as a punishment, the brand
Of having wished to change their place.

[Baudelaire, *CP* III]

Meditation

[after Baudelaire]

BE good, my Sorrow: hush now: settle down.
You sighed for dusk, and now it comes: look there!
A denser atmosphere obscures the town,
To some restoring peace, to others care.

While the lewd multitude, like hungry beasts,
By pleasure scourged (no thug so fierce as he!)
Go forth to seek remorse among their feasts—
Come, take my hand; escape from them with me.

From balconies of sky, around us yet,
Lean the dead years in fashions that have ceased.
Out of the depth of waters smiles Regret.

The sun sinks moribund beneath an arch,
And like a long shroud rustling from the East,
Hark, Love, the gentle Night is on the march.

[Baudelaire, *CP* III]

The Louse Catchers

[after Rimbaud]

WHEN the child's brow, with torment flushing red,
Implores white dreams to shed their hazy veils,
Two sisters, tall and fair, approach his bed
Whose fingers glint with silver-pointed nails.

They seat him by a window, where the blue   5
Air bathes a sheaf of flowers: with rhythms calm,
Into his heavy hair where falls the dew,
Prowl their long fingers terrible in charm.

He hears their breathing whistle in long sighs
Flowering with ghostly pollen; and the hiss   10
Of spittle on the lips withdrawn, where dies
From time to time the fancy of a kiss.

Brushing cool cheeks their feathered lashes flick
The perfumed silences: through drifting veils
He hears their soft electric fingers click   15
The death of tiny lice with regal nails.

Drowsed in the deep wines of forgetfulness,
Delirious harmonies his spirit hears
And to the rhythm of their slow caress
Wavers and pauses on the verge of tears.   20

[P, FR, CP I, CP III]

Love Song – At St Simeon's
shrine I sat down to wait – Mindinho

AT St Simeon's shrine I sat down to wait,
The waves came nearer, the waves grew great,
   As I was awaiting my lover,
   As I was awaiting my lover!

There at St Simeon's shrine by the altar,   5
Greater and nearer, the waves did not falter,
   As I was awaiting my lover,
   As I was awaiting my lover!
As the waves drew nearer and greater grew,
There was no steersman nor rower in view,   10
   As I was awaiting my lover,
   As I was awaiting my lover!
The waves of the high sea nearer flow
There is no steersman, I cannot row
   As I am awaiting my lover,   15
   As I am awaiting my lover!
There is no steersman nor rower, and I
In the high sea in my beauty must die,
   As I am awaiting my lover,
   As I am awaiting my lover!   20
There is no steersman, no rower am I
And in the high sea my beauty must die,
   As I am awaiting my lover,
   As I am awaiting my lover.

[CP III]

Re-encounter—Joaquim Paço d'Arcos

THE jetty with its old wormeaten planks,
The cheerless sand-dunes and the ancient fort,
The desert that advances on the sea
Peppering the poor city with its yellow dust
And burying it in sand.   5

The vegetable gardens of Giraul,
A timid streak of green in sandy wastes,
The withered flowerbeds, burnt and dried,
By the fierce sun of Africa,
Destroy, when re-encountered thus, the image   10
Of the lush park which memory retained.

The little garden in the ctiy,
Without its bandstand now,
But with its filing spectres,
Its long, interminable files of spectres . . .   15
Miss Blond out walking with her childish charges.
'Tiger', the dog, so mute and mild and sleepy.
The negroes with submissive, startled looks,
Walking with fettered feet
Through a street of mud-built huts and yielding earth.   20
Miss Blond no longer takes the children walking,
Tall, noble 'Tiger' died of ripe old age,
The natives long ago destroyed their fetters,
Only the spectres have remained
Where they were left. They, only, populate   25
The memory and inhabit the town,
With their faint, beloved voices,
With their lost voices
In the deserted House, which now the desert
Covers with dust, and in this life, which time   30
Is covering with its dust,
In death, in memory, in death . . .

                                                    [CP III]

Counsel—Manuel Bandeira

THE world is pitiless and lewdly jeers
All tragedy. Anticipate your loss.
Weep silently, in secret. Hide your tears,
So to become accustomed to your cross.

Alone grief can ennoble us. She only   5
Is grand and pure. Then learn to love her now—
To be your muse, when you are left and lonely,
And lay the last green laurels on your brow.

123

She will be sent from Heaven. The seraphic
Language she speaks in, you should learn, for she   10
Can talk no other in your daily traffic,

When you receive her to replace your bride.
Pray humbly, too, to God, that she may be
A constant, kind companion at your side.

[May 1952. *CP* II, *CP* III]

INDEX OF TITLES AND
FIRST LINES

127